8.6

THE GREAT ALASKA EARTHQUAKE

MARCH 27, 1964

Good Friday
27 March 1964

—Suddenly, the earth rocked and rolled—
Seismographs throughout the Pacific area registered a magnitude from 8.2 to 8.7 on the Richter scale. A quake of this magnitude, according to seismologists, would result in the following destruction:

· Few masonry structures, if any, remain standing
· Bridges destroyed
· Broad fissures in ground
· Underground pipelines completely out of service
· Earth slumps and land slips in soft ground
· Rails bend greatly

And thus, this was the picture of devastation throughout much of Alaska following the Good Friday earthquake and seismic waves that came in its wake.

Quake Flattens Alaska C[i]

Missoulian-Sentinel

Britons Relieved By U.N.

Quake Shock Felt Here

Board Will Rectify Assessment Errors

LIFE

April 10, 1964

In Color:
EARTHQUAKE
IN ALASKA

The New York Times.

LATE CITY EDITION

SCORES PERISH IN ALASKA QUAKE
AND TIDAL WAVES ON WEST COAST;
ANCHORAGE SUFFERS WORST LOSS

WHITE HOUSE ACTS

Saud Stripped of Power.
Faisal Takes Full Control

APRIL 10 · 1964 · 25

The Alaska Earthquake made headlines around the
world and many national magazines.

8.6

THE GREAT ALASKA EARTHQUAKE

MARCH 27, 1964

by Stan Cohen

The Good Friday earthquake's epicenter is believed to be just north of Prince William Sound, 12-1/2 miles below the surface in the vicinity of College Fiord. COE

PICTORIAL HISTORIES PUBLISHING COMPANY

LIBRARY OF CONGRESS
CATALOG CARD NO. 95-67027

ISBN 0-929521-96-X

First Printing: March 1995
Second Printing: March 1997
Third Printing: March 2000
Fourth Printing: February 2003
Fifth Printing: February 2005
Sixth Printing: February 2007
Seventh Printing: February 2008

Printed by Jostens, Visalia, California

FRONT COVER PHOTOS:

Railroad destruction. COE
4th Avenue subsidence in Anchorage. AMHA
Fishing fleet destruction in Seward. COE

PICTORIAL HISTORIES PUBLISHING CO., INC.
713 South Third Street West, Missoula, MT 59801
PHONE (406) 549-8488, FAX (406) 728-9280
EMAIL phpc@montana.com
WEBSITE pictorialhistoriespublishing.com

INTRODUCTION

Seismologists describe an earthquake with a recording on the Richter Scale greater than 8.2 as follows: "Few masonry structures, if any remain standing; bridges destroyed; broad fissures in ground; underground pipe lines completely out of service; earth slump and land slips in soft ground; and rails bend greatly."

The Good Friday earthquake that struck southern Alaska at 5:36 p.m. on March 27, 1964, had a registered magnitude on the Richter Scale of 8.2 to 8.7, the most devastating quake on record in North America.*

All the above damages, including great tsunamis and seiche waves, occurred in the affected Alaska area and along the West Coast of the United States. It was a period of extraordinary land shifts and geologic changes. The quake was felt throughout the world with well fluctuations and small wave activity in lakes on every continent.

The earthquake is typical of Mother Nature's affliction on the "Great Land." The state has large forest fires, volcanic activity, glacial movement and massive floods. The environmental aspects of the "Land" are awesome, wondrous and at times devastating.

Earthquakes are a standard occurrence in Alaska, along what is commonly called the "Ring of Fire," a band that runs the length of the Aleutian Islands around Cook Inlet, Prince William Sound, down the panhandle, and along the west coast of Canada and the United States. Earthquakes in the higher magnitudes are common in the Aleutian Chain, but the remoteness and lack of structure and population centers preclude much damage from them.

The quake in south-central Alaska was of devastating proportions. It was amazing that the death toll was not greater than 114, considering the magnitude and great seismic waves that occurred. Alaskans responded in record time and numbers to help their fellow citizens. Help poured in from the lower 48 states as well. It was a major catastrophe that remains with the citizens of Alaska today.

Most of the information in this book was taken from the numerous reports compiled and published by the United States Geological Survey shortly after the quake (see bibliography). The photographs were gathered from a number of sources in Alaska and California and were chosen to portray the vast destructive nature of the quake and subsequent tsunamis and seiche waves. The photographs are credited to their source and photographer when known.

The text is short. I have tried to let the photos tell the story. For those who need a detailed explanation of the geologic and human aspects of the disaster, I suggest that you pursue the bibliographic sources and other material that is available.

Stan Cohen

* Some seismographs actually recorded readings up to 9.2 on the Richter scale.

Acknowledgments

Many people helped in my gathering of photographs and information for this book. I would particularly like to thank Margaret Weatherly of Reeve Aleutian Airways in Anchorage; John Killoren and Pat Richardson of the Alaska District, U.S. Army Corps of Engineers, Anchorage; Diane Brenner of The Anchorage Museum of History and Art; the staff of the Command Historian, Elmendorf Air Force Base, Anchorage; Marilyn Kwock, Juneau; India Spartz and Ellen Fitzgerald of The Alaska State Library, Alaska Historical Collections, Juneau; Alice Ryser of The Kodiak Historical Society; Guy Powell, Kodiak; Gretchen Lake and staff of the Alaska & Polar Regions Department, The Elmer E. Rasmuson Library, University of Alaska, Fairbanks; staff of the Valdez Museum & Archives; Wallace Griffin of The Crescent City Printing Co., Inc., Crescent City, California; The Crescent City Chamber of Commerce and The Del Norte Historical Society, Crescent City, California.

Table of Contents

Photo Sources

COE—U.S. Army Corps of Engineers, Anchorage
DNHS—Del Norte Historical Society, Crescent City, Calif.
VM—Valdez Museum & Archive, Valdez
AMHA—Anchorage Museum of History & Art
ASL—Alaska State Library, Juneau
UAA—University of Alaska, Alaska & Polar Regions Dept.,
    The Elmer E. Rasmuson Library, Fairbanks
USA—U.S. Army Archives
USAF—U.S. Air Force, Elmendorf Air Force Base, Anchorage
GP—Guy Powell Collection, Kodiak

Alaska Earthquake Statistics

· Alaska has 11 percent of the World's earthquakes.
· Alaska has 52 percent of all the earthquakes in the United States.
· Three of the six largest earthquakes in the United States were in Alaska.
· Seven of the 10 largest earthquakes in the United States were in Alaska.

Since 1900, Alaska has had an average of:
· One magnitude eight or larger earthquake every 13 years.
· One magnitude seven to eight earthquake every year.
· Four and a half, if it's possible to have a half magnitude, six to seven earthquakes per year.
· Twenty magnitude five to six earthquakes per year.
· Ninety magnitude four to five earthquakes per year.

GEOLOGIC TERMS

1. Earthquake—Groups of elastic waves propagating in the earth, set up by a transient disturbance of the elastic equilibrium of a portion of the earth.

2. Epicenter—The point on the earth's surface directly above the focus of an earthquake.

3. Fault—A fracture of fracture zone along which there has been displacement of the sides relative to one another parallel to the fracture. The displacement may be a few inches or many miles.

4. Fault Block—A mass bounded on at least two opposite sides by faults; it may be elevated or depressed relatively to the adjoining region, or it may be elevated relatively to the region on one side and depressed relatively to that on the other.

5. Graben—A block, generally long compared to its width, that has been downthrown along faults relative to the rocks on either side.

6. Seiche—A periodic oscillation of a body of water whose period is determined by the resonant characteristics of the containing basin as controlled by its physical dimensions. These periods generally range from a few minutes to an hour or more. Applies to lakes, harbors, bays and oceans.

7. Seismic—Pertaining to, characteristic of, or produced by earthquakes, or earth vibration, as seismic disturbances.

8. Subsidence—A sinking of a large part of the earth's crust.

9. Tectonic—Of, pertaining to, or designating the rock structure and external forms resulting from the deformation of the earth's crust. As applied to earthquakes, it is used to describe shocks not due to volcanic action or to collapse of caverns or landslides.

10. Tsunami—A great sea wave produced by a submarine earthquake or volcanic eruption.

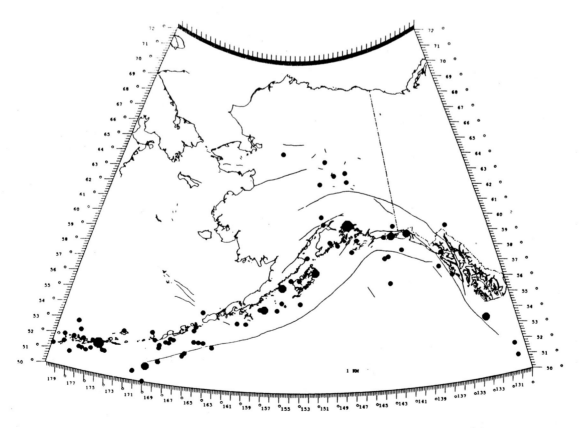

Earthquakes of magnitude 7.0 and larger in Alaska, 1899 to 1988. The three sizes of dots represent earthquakes of magnitudes 7-8, 8-9 and above 9, respectively. Lines indicate faults. EARTHQUAKE ALASKA—ARE WE PREPARED?, U.S. GEOLOGICAL SURVEY, OPEN-FILE REPORT 94-218, 1994

TSUNAMI — THE GREAT WAVE

The phenomenon we call "tsunami" is a series of traveling ocean waves of extremely long length and period. In the deep ocean their length from crest to crest may be more than a hundred miles. Their height from trough to crest measures only a few feet. They cannot be felt aboard ships in deep water, and they cannot be seen from the air. But the kinetic energy—the energy of movement—created by a tsunami is impressive: a tsunami "feels the bottom" even in the deepest ocean. It appears that the progress of this imperceptible series of waves represents the movement of the entire vertical section of ocean through which the tsunami passes. In the deep ocean, they may reach speeds of 600 miles per hour.

As the tsunami enters the shoaling water of coastlines, the velocity of its waves diminishes and wave height increases. The arrival of a tsunami is often (but not always) heralded by a gradual recession of coastal water when the trough precedes the initial crest; or trumpeted by a rise in water level of about one-half the amplitude of the subsequent recession. This is nature's warning that more severe tsunami waves are approaching. It is a warning to be heeded, for tsunami waves can crest to height of more than 100 feet, and will strike with devastating force.

Tsunamis are believed to originate as vertically displaced columns of ocean water, but the displacing agent has not been positively identified. Seismic or volcanic alterations of the ocean floor, provided they impart some vertical movement to the water column, may cause tsunamis. It has also been postulated that submarine avalanches on the slopes of the Pacific trenches produce tsunamis.

Some investigators have turned to long-period ground waves which sometimes accompany large earthquakes as possible generators of tsunamis. Deformation of the sea floor as these waves travel across it could reach sufficient amplitude to produce large water surface displacements, particularly in the region of troughs or trenches. It is possible that long-period earthquake waves generate tsunamis by setting up resonant oscillations of trench water.

Although it has been established that a relationship exists between seismic or volcanic disturbances and tsunamis, the nature of this relationship is not well-defined. Tsunami magnitude appears to be a function of earthquake magnitude and depth, water depth in the region of tsunami generation, extent and velocity of crustal deformation, and efficiency of energy transfer from the earth's crust to sea water. However, the specific effect upon tsunamis of these independent factors is imperfectly understood.

The speed of tsunamis varies with water depth. This relationship permits prediction of tsunami arrival times at all points in the Pacific Ocean area. But no definite correlation has been possible between the configuration of specific regions of the ocean floor and tsunami configuration in those regions. For example, it is not clear why a tsunami's waves may be negligible size at one point along the coast, and of much larger proportions at other coastal points. Nor is it possible to predict whether the destructive component of a tsunami will lie in its powerful surge across a beach, or in a gradual rising of sea level followed by a rapid draining back to sea.

Thus it is uncertain what shape a tsunami will assume at specific locations, or how it will accomplish its destructive work. Regarding tsunamis, exceptions are the rule.

The following information was taken from the U.S. Geological Survey pamphlet by Louis C. Pakiser, U.S. Government Printing Office, 1988.

Earthquakes in History

The scientific study of earthquakes is comparatively new.

Until the 18th century few factual descriptions of earthquakes were recorded, and the natural cause of quakes was little understood. Many people believed that an earthquake was a massive punishment and a warning to the unrepentant. A 16th century scholar, for example, suggested that statues of Mercury and Saturn be placed on each wall of buildings to protect against earthquakes. Those who did look for natural causes often reached fanciful conclusions; one popular theory was that earthquakes were caused by air rushing out of caverns deep in the Earth's interior.

An early earthquake for which we have detailed descriptive information occurred on Nov. 1, 1755, in the vicinity of Lisbon, Portugal. Shocks from the quake were felt in many parts of the world. In some parts of the United States chandeliers rattled, and in Europe buildings trembled.

After the quake, Portuguese priests were asked to document their observations. Their records, still preserved, represent the first systematic attempt to investigate an earthquake and its effects. Since then, detailed records have been kept of almost every major quake.

The most widely felt earthquakes in the recorded history of North America were a series that occurred in 1811-12 near New Madrid, Mo. The shocks started Dec. 16, 1811, and continued intermittently for two days. Large shocks followed on Jan. 23, 1812, and again on February 7. The largest of these quakes was felt over an area of two million square miles—from Canada to the Gulf of Mexico and from the Rocky Mountains to the Atlantic Ocean. Because the most intense affects were in a sparsely populated region, the destruction of human life and property was slight. If this quake occurred in the same area today, it probably would cause severe damage to many cities in the Central Mississippi Valley.

The San Francisco earthquake of 1906 was one of the most destructive in the recorded history of North America—the quake and the fire that followed killed nearly 700 people and left the city in ruins. The Alaska earthquake of March 27, 1964, however, was of greater magnitude than the San Francisco quake; it released perhaps twice as much energy and was felt over an area of almost 500,000 square miles. The ground motion near the epicenter was so violent that the tops of some trees were snapped off. One hundred and fourteen people (some as far away as California) died as a result of this earthquake, but loss of life and property would have been far greater had Alaska been more densely populated.

Locations of Earthquakes

Most earthquakes occur in areas bordering the Pacific Ocean. This circum-Pacific belt, called the "ring of fire," includes the Pacific coasts of North and South America, the Aleutians, Japan, Southeast Asia and Australasia. Half a million people within this area have lost their lives because of earthquakes, and property valued in billions of dollars has been severely damaged or destroyed.

The United States has experienced less destruction than other countries located in this ring of fire, but millions of Americans live in potential quake areas. Large parts of the Western United States are known to be particularly vulnerable. Nuclear reactors, great dams, schools, and high-rise apartments and other housing developments are being planned and built in places where the danger of major earthquakes is ever present. This has created an urgent need for more information on the nature, and causes and effects of earthquakes.

Scientists, including those of the U.S. Geological Survey's National Center for Earthquake Research in Menlo Park, Calif., are studying the causes of earthquakes in hopes of finding methods of prediction and of developing practices that will reduce their destructive effects.

Nature of Earthquakes

An earthquake is the oscillatory, sometimes violent movement of the Earth's surface that follows a release of energy in the Earth's crust. This energy can be generated by a sudden dislocation of segments of the crust, by a volcanic eruption, or even by man-made explosions. Most of the destructive quakes, however, are caused by dislocations of the crust. When subjected to deep-seated forces (whose origins and natures are largely unknown) the crust may first bend and then, when the stress exceeds the strength of the rocks, break and "snap" to a new position. In the process of breaking, vibrations called "seismic waves" are generated. These waves travel from the source of the earthquake to more distant places along the surface and through the Earth at varying speeds depending on the medium through which they move. Some of the vibrations are of high enough frequency to be audible, while others are of very low frequency—actually many seconds or minutes between swings. These vibrations cause the entire planet to quiver or ring like a bell or a tuning fork.

A *fault* is a fracture in the Earth's crust along which two blocks of the crust have slipped with respect to each other. One crustal block may move horizontally in one direction while the block facing it moves in the opposite direction, or one block may move upward while the other moves downward. Faults are distinguished by the kinds of movements that characterize them. Movement along California's famous San Andreas Fault is predominantly horizontal, and the fault is called a *strike-slip* fault. A fault in which the movement is vertical is called a *dip-slip* fault. Along many faults, movement is both horizontal and vertical.

Geologists have found that earthquakes tend to reoccur along faults, which reflect zones of weakness in the Earth's crust. The fact that a fault zone has recently experienced a quake offers no assurance that enough stress has been relieved to prevent another one.

The *focal depth* of an earthquake is the depth from the Earth's surface to the region (*focus*) where its energy originates. Earthquakes with focal depths from the surface to about 60 kilometers (38 miles) are classified as shallow. Those with focal depths from 60 to 300 kilometers (38 to 188 miles) are classified as intermediate. The focus of deep earthquakes may reach depths as far as 700 kilometers (440 miles).

The focuses of most earthquakes are concentrated in the crust and upper mantle. Compared to a depth of about 4,000 miles to the center of the Earth's core, earthquakes can be considered to originate in relatively shallow parts of the Earth's interior. Earthquakes in California along the San Andreas and associated faults have shallow focal depths; for most the depth is less than 10 miles. During the past 100 years, Earth movements have occurred along more than half the entire length of the San Andreas Fault and the rupture itself is visible at the land surface in many places.

Very shallow earthquakes are probably caused by fracturing of the brittle rock in the crust or by internal stresses that overcome the frictional resistance locking opposite sides of a fault. The immediate cause of an intermediate or deep earthquake is not yet fully understood.

The *epicenter* of an earthquake is the point on the Earth's surface directly above the focus. The location of an earthquake is commonly described by the geographic position of its epicenter and by its focal depth.

Earthquakes beneath the ocean floor sometimes generate immense sea waves or "tsunamis" (Japan's dread "huge wave"). These waves travel across the ocean at speeds as great as 960 kilometers per hour (600 miles per hour) and may be 15 meters (50 feet) high or higher by the time they reach the shore. During the 1964 Alaska quake, tsunamis engulfing coastal areas caused most of the destruction at Kodiak, Cordova, and Seward and caused severe damage along the west coast of North America, particularly at Crescent City, Calif. Some waves raced across the ocean to the coasts of Japan.

Water levels in artesian wells fluctuate as seismic waves travel through the rock layers that hold the water. During passage of seismic waves from a large earthquake, water levels in some wells fluctuate wildly, not only in the immediate vicinity of the earthquake but also at great distances from it. The water level change may be long-lasting or even permanent. The Alaska quake appears to have caused changes in wells in many areas, both local and remote. Water levels in wells in New Orleans, La., for example, rose and fell as a result of the quake.

Landslides triggered by earthquakes often cause more destruction than the shocks themselves. During the 1964 Alaska quake, shock-induced landslides devastated the Turnagain Heights residential development and many downtown areas in Anchorage. An observer gave a vivid report of the breakup of the unstable Earth materials in the Turnagain Heights region:

"I got out of my car, ran northward toward my driveway, and then saw that the bluff had broken back approximately 300 feet southward from its original edge. Additional slumping of the bluff caused me to return to my car and back southward approximately 180 feet to the corner of McCollie and Turnagain Parkway. The bluff slowly broke until the corner of Turnagain Parkway and McCollie had slumped northward."

Measurement of Earthquakes

The vibrations produced by earthquakes are

detected, recorded, and measured by instruments called seismographs. The zig-zag line made by a seismograph, called a "seismogram," reflects the varying amplitude of the vibrations by responding to the motion of the ground surface beneath the instrument. From the data expressed in seismograms, the time, the epicenter, and the focal depth of an earthquake can be determined, and estimates can be made of the amount of energy that was released.

The two general types of vibrations produced by earthquakes are *surface waves* which travel along the Earth's surface and *body waves* which travel through the Earth. Surface waves usually have the strongest vibrations and probably cause most of the damage done by quakes.

Body waves are of two types, *compressional* and *shear*. Both types of body waves pass through the Earth's interior from the focus of an earthquake to distant points on the surface, but only compressional waves travel through the Earth's molten core. Because compressional waves travel at great speeds and ordinarily reach the surface first, they are often called "primary waves" or simply "P" waves. P waves push tiny particles of Earth material directly ahead of them or displace the particles directly behind their line of travel.

Shear waves do not travel as rapidly through the Earth's crust and mantle. Because they ordinarily reach the surface later, they are called "secondary" or "S" waves. Instead of affecting material directly behind or ahead of their line of travel, shear waves displace material at right angles to their path and are therefore sometimes called "transverse" waves.

The first indication of an earthquake will often be a sharp thud—signaling the arrival of compressional waves. This will be followed by the shear waves and then the "ground roll" caused by the surface waves. A geologist who was at Valdez, Alaska, during the 1964 earthquake described this phenomenon:

The first tremors were hard enough to stop a moving person and shock waves were immediately noticeable on the surface of the ground. These shock waves continued with a rather long frequency which gave the observer an impression of a rolling feeling rather than abrupt hard jolts. After about one minute the amplitude or strength of the shock waves increased in intensity, and failures in buildings as well as the frozen ground surface began to occur...After about 3-1/2 minutes the severe shock waves ended and people began to react as expected.

The times of arrival of compressional and shear waves at selected seismograph stations throughout the world indicate where and when the earthquake occurred and, sometimes, its focal depth. The recorded amplitudes of seismic waves indicate the amount of energy released by the quake.

The severity of an earthquake can be expressed in several ways. The *magnitude* of a quake, as expressed by the *Richter Scale*, is a measure of the amplitude of the seismic waves and is related to the amount of energy released—an amount that can be estimated from seismograph recordings. The *intensity*, as expressed by the *Modified Mercalli Scale*, is a subjective measure which describes how severe a shock was felt at a particular location. Damage or loss of life and property is another, and ultimately the most important, measure of a quake's severity.

The Richter Scale, named after Dr. Charles F. Richter of the California Institute of Technology, is the best known scale for measuring the magnitude of earthquakes. The scale is logarithmic so that a recording of seven, for example, indicates a disturbance with ground motion 10 times as large as a recording of six. A quake of magnitude two is the smallest quake normally felt by humans. Earthquakes with a Richter value of six or more are commonly considered major in magnitude.

The Modified Mercalli Scale expresses the intensity of an earthquake's effects in a given locality in values ranging from I to XII. The most commonly used adaptation covers the range of intensity from the condition of "I—Not felt except by a very few under especially favorable conditions," to "XII—Damage total. Lines of sight and level are distorted. Objects thrown upward into the air." Evaluation of quake intensity can be made only after eyewitness reports and results of field investigations are studied and interpreted. The maximum intensity experienced in the Alaska earthquake of 1964 was X; the San Francisco quake of 1906 reached a maximum intensity of XI.

Earthquakes of large magnitude do not necessarily cause the most intense surface effects. The effect in a given region depends to a large degree on local surface and subsurface geologic conditions. An area underlain by unstable ground (sand, clay, or other unconsolidated materials), for example, is likely to experience more noticeable effects than an area equally distant from a quake's epicenter but underlain by firm ground such as granite.

A quake's destructiveness depends on many factors. In addition to magnitude, these include the focal depth, the distance from the epicenter, local geologic conditions, and the design of buildings and other works of man. The extent of damage also depends on the density of population and construction in the area shaken by the quake.

The Alaska earthquake of 1964 demonstrated wide variations in its effects. The town of Whittier, built on firm granite, suffered little damage from the seismic waves despite the fact that it was close to the epicenter. Whittier did experience great destruction and the loss of 13 lives from the enormous seawaves produced by submarine landslides, however. In Anchorage, much farther from the epicenter, damage was selective; the greatest destruction occurred in areas where homes and other buildings were constructed near unstable slopes underlain by clay and other unconsolidated materials.

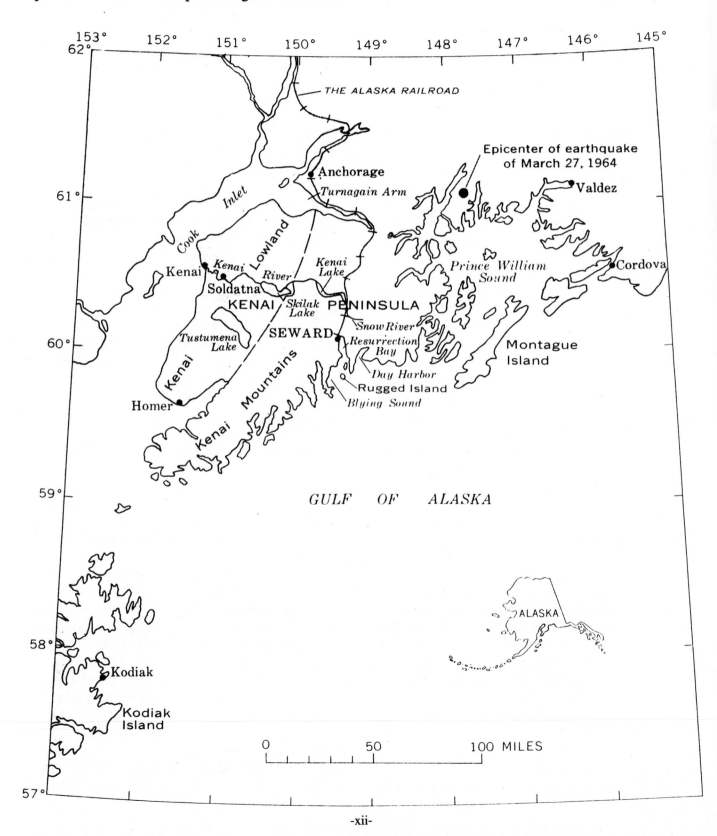

ANCHORAGE

The Mt. McKinley Building on Denali Street between
Third and Fourth avenues was heavily damaged. COE

Anchorage, is about 80 miles west-northwest of the epicenter of the earthquake. Because of its size, Anchorage bore the brunt of property damage from the quake; it sustained greater losses than all the rest of Alaska combined. Damage was caused by direct seismic vibration, by ground cracks and by landslides. Direct seismic vibration affected chiefly multistory buildings and buildings having large floor areas, probably because of the long period and large amplitude of the seismic waves reaching Anchorage. Most small buildings were spared. Ground cracks caused capricious damage throughout the Anchorage Lowland. Cracking was most prevalent near the heads or within landslides but was also widespread elsewhere. Landslides themselves caused the most devastating damage.

Total earthquake damage to property in the Anchorage area has not been fully evaluated and perhaps will never be fully known. Nine lives are reported to have been lost—five in the downtown area, three at Turnagain Heights, and one at the International Airport. In less than five minutes, more than 2,000 people, including apartment dwellers, were made homeless, according to press estimates. The loss of life was less in Anchorage than in some of the small coastal towns, where many people were killed by sea waves.

The Office of Emergency Planning estimated the total damage to Alaska at about $537,600,000, of which about 60 percent was sustained by the Anchorage area. The school system was hard hit. Early estimates of damage came to about $3.86 million. Classes were not in session, fortunately, so the buildings were empty. Twenty of the 26 schools in Anchorage were soon back in operation. West Anchorage High School, however, was severely damaged by seismic vibration. Government Hill Grade School, astride a landslide, was nearly a total loss, although plans have been made to salvage an intact part of the building outside the slide for use other than as a school. Denali Grade School was damaged by ground cracks and was closed indefinitely, pending damage evaluation and repair.

In downtown Anchorage (the L Street and Fourth Avenue landslide areas), about 30 blocks of dwellings and commercial buildings were destroyed or severely damaged. A new six-story apartment building, the Four Seasons, was razed. A new five-story J.C. Penney department store was damaged beyond repair by seismic shaking and had to be torn down. Many automobiles in the downtown area were struck by falling debris. Twin 14-story apartment buildings, though a mile apart, sustained massive, nearly identical vibratory damage, much of it in response to vertical shearing forces caused by oscillation. Many other multistory or large-area buildings were severely damaged.

Water mains and gas, sewer, telephone and electric systems were disrupted. Total damage to utilities has been estimated at about $15 million.

Fourth Avenue in Anchorage before the quake. COE

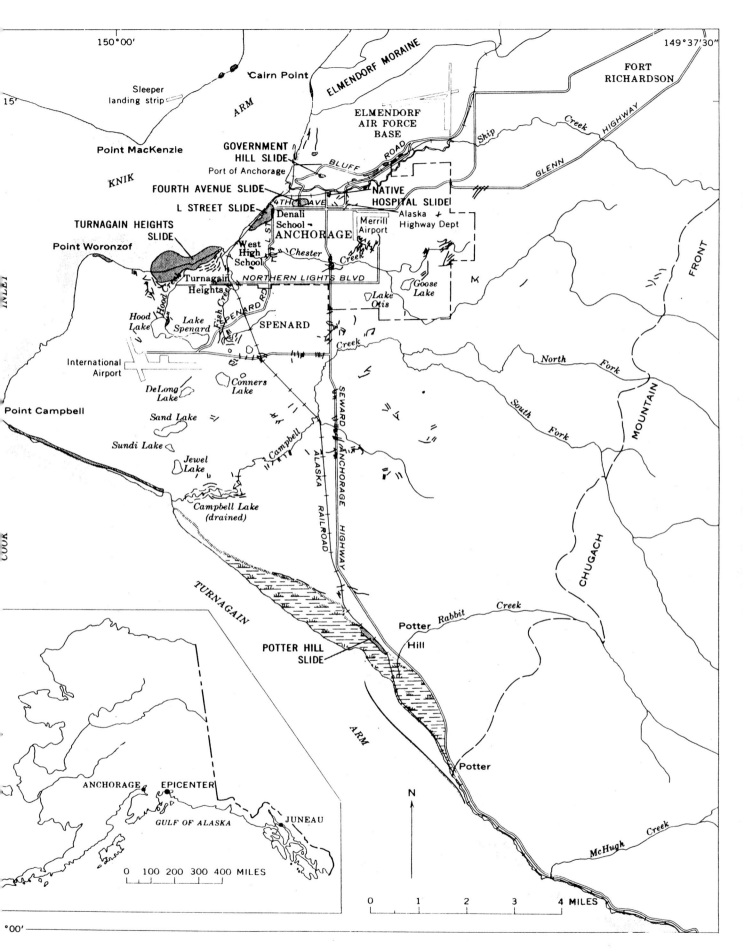

Generalized map of Anchorage and vicinity, showing locations of major landslides and ground cracks. USGS

The Downtown Area

The downtown area. Fourth Avenue looking east (top), pre-quake, and Fourth Avenue looking west (bottom), post-quake, COE

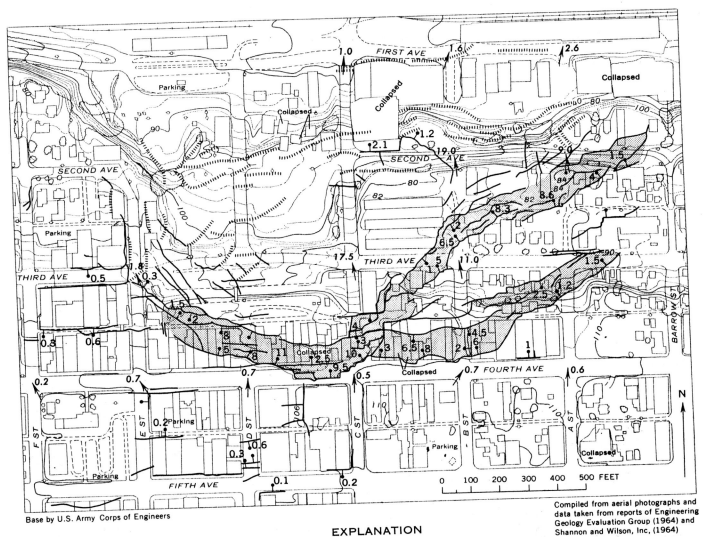

Base by U.S. Army Corps of Engineers

Compiled from aerial photographs and
data taken from reports of Engineering
Geology Evaluation Group (1964) and
Shannon and Wilson, Inc, (1964)

EXPLANATION

1.5
Fracture, showing downthrown
side and displacement in feet

Pressure ridge

Graben

9.0
Lateral displacement of
bench mark, in feet.
New position at point
of arrow. No appre-
ciable movement since
earthquake

Fourth Avenue landslide area. USGS

**Fourth Avenue at L
Street in the summer of
1964. The destroyed
buildings have not yet
been removed but the
street has been brought
back to grade again. The
Anchorage Westward
Hotel is in the back-
ground. It sustained
considerable damage.** COE

Fifth Avenue and B Street with the Penney's building on the left. COE

COE

The year old J.C. Penney Building on Fifth Avenue was a total loss. Its five stories were built out of reinforced-concrete, shear walls on three sides and a curtain wall of precast panels on its north side. Rotational motion caused the west support wall at the second-story level to shear off, collapsing all the floors. The northeast corner of the building collapsed and most of the precast panels on the north face fell to the street. The station wagon in front of the building was flattened to a height of three feet and the occupant, who was attempting to move it, was killed. The building was torn down and replaced by the present downtown structure.

The J.C. Penney Building

Fourth Avenue

View along the north side of east Fourth Avenue (bottom, right) showing the dramatic collapse of the Denali Theater Building into the graben. A close-up view of the theater (top, left). The theater was filled with children at the time of the earthquake. An orderly evacuation occurred after the quake ended. AMHA, #B76·118·13 & B69·11·14

View looking east along Fourth Avenue (bottom) and looking west (top) on the north side of the street that collapsed into a 10-foot graben. The tall building in the background is the 14-story Anchorage Westward Hotel which sustained considerable interior structural damage. COE

Steve McCutcheon's well-known photo shop on Fourth Avenue was a total wreck. His brother Stanley is shown examining the damage. AMHA STEVE McCUTCHEON COLLECTION #16007

Damage between Third and Fourth avenues. COE

The Four Seasons Apartment Building at West Ninth Avenue and M Street was a spectacular total loss. It was designed for year-round luxury living, but didn't survive its first season. The building was nearing completion at the time of the earthquake, but fortunately it was not yet occupied—it collapsed in a pile of rubble. It was a six-story lift-slab reinforced-concrete building with two central poured-in-place cores, one for a stairwell and one for an elevator. The floor slabs were torn loose from shear heads on the structural-steel columns and pulled away from keyways in the stairwell and elevator cores. Some dowels connecting the slabs to the cores broke; others were pulled free. COE

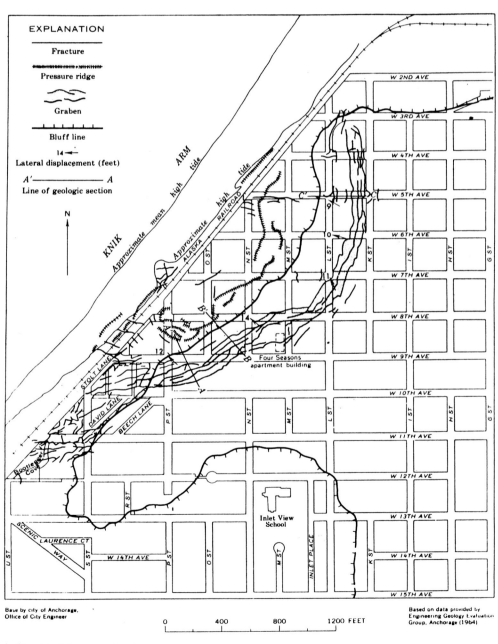

EXPLANATION

———— Fracture

————————— Pressure ridge

〰〰〰 Graben

———— Bluff line

14◄— Lateral displacement (feet)

A'————————A Line of geologic section

N

Base by city of Anchorage, Office of City Engineer

Based on data provided by Engineering Geology Evaluation Group, Anchorage (1964)

0   400   800   1200 FEET

L Street slide area, Anchorage. USGS

-11-

Ground cracks were prominent in many parts of the Anchorage area. COE

The First Federal Savings and Loan Building at the northwest corner of Fifth Avenue and C Street was heavily damaged, although the east and south walls, mainly of glass, sustained little breakage. The building was eventually repaired. COE

Books were thrown askew in all directions at the downtown Loussac Library. AMHA

The Mt. McKinley Building, a 14-story reinforced-concrete apartment building, is located on Denali Street between Third and Fourth avenues. Most of the damage to this building was in the form of X-shaped shear cracks in the spandrel beams and to vertical piers which sheared horizontally, mainly at the third-story level. One resident reported that after 30 seconds of trembling motion, the building experienced about two minutes of violent jarring, in which it seemed to sway eight to 10 feet horizontally and one to two feet vertically. The building is now called the McKay Building. COE

Extensive damage occurred just below the downtown area. The tall building in the background is the Anchorage Westward Hotel.

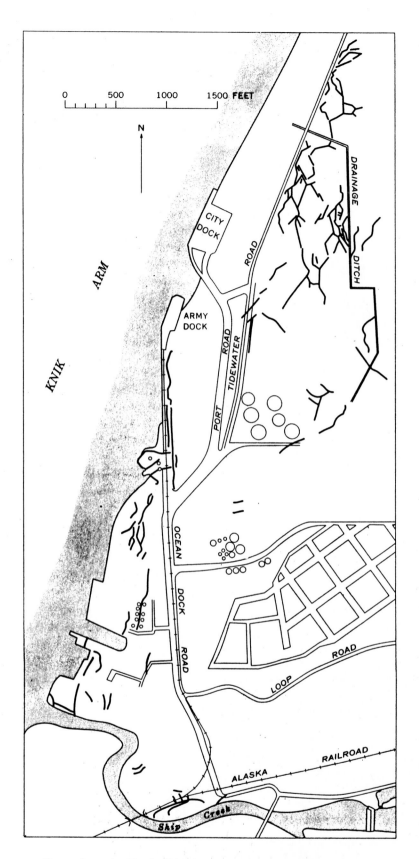

Ground cracks, Port of Anchorage and vicinity. Many of these cracks spouted mud, particularly those east of City Dock. USGS

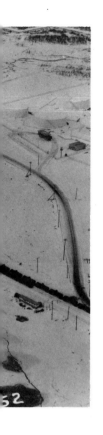

Much of the damage in the Port of Anchorage area was caused by ground displacements along fractures, but some damage is attributable to direct seismic shaking. The main pier lurched laterally five to 19 inches. Large longitudinal cracks and several transverse ones opened up, and the walls of several buildings were cracked. All four gantry cranes were damaged. Steel piles penetrated the deck of a subordinate pier. Approach roads and railroads settled as much as 18 inches. Two cement-storage tanks were toppled, one at the property of the Permanente Cement Co. at the entrance to the U.S. Army Dock and one at the Alaska Aggregate Corp. facility just north of Ship Creek. Oil-storage tanks in the dock area were mostly superficially damaged, but some tanks were bulged outward at the bottom, probably by rocking and pounding back and forth as the contents sloshed to and fro. ASL, U.S. ARMY COE COLLECTION, PCA 100-54

Bent I beam at the Cordova Building, a six-story building at the northeast corner of Sixth Avenue and Cordova Street. Damage was mainly in the first story. A corner support column failed and the exterior reinforced-concrete curtain walls sheared at the top of the basement. The center column in the south wall buckled and the reinforced-concrete stair and elevator shaft sheared at the first story. The penthouse also collapsed. AMHA

The Native Hospital landslide disrupted part of the grounds of the Alaska Native Service Hospital and wrecked a fuel-storage tank at the foot of the bluff. It involved about four acres of land and 360,000 cubic yards of earth. The hospital was slightly damaged by ground fractures. The scar of an older landslide was transected by the March 27 slide. COE

This damaged I beam, on display at the Anchorage Museum of History and Art, is from the Cordova Building, now called The Olympic Building at the corner of 6th and Cordova.

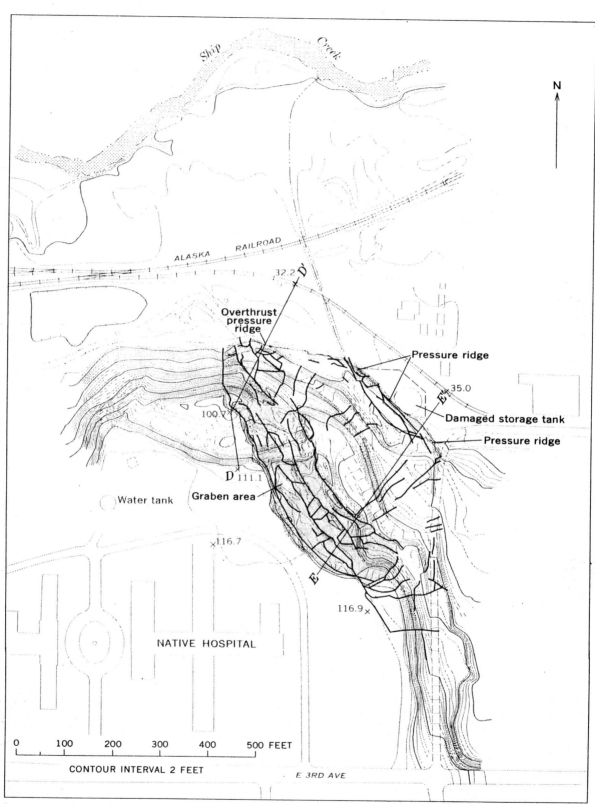

Native Hospital slide area, Anchorage. usgs

The new Anchorage Cold Storage building at the base of C Street was in shambles. ALS, U.S. ARMY COE, PCA 100-149

The Hillside Apartments were on the south side of Sixteenth Avenue between G and H streets on a bluff overlooking Chester Creek. Damaged beyond repair, they were demolished. This was a split-level building, five stories high on the south side and three stories high on the street side. It had a post-and-lintel frame with steel-pipe columns, rolled-steel beams and concrete floor slabs on steel joists. Walls were unreinforced hollow concrete block. The building was sheared in an east-west direction at the third-story level on the south side and in the lower two stories on the north side—the upper stories lurched west relative to the lower stories. Seemingly, no provision had been made for resistance to strong lateral seismic stress. AMHA, VIRGINIA CHANEY COLLECTION

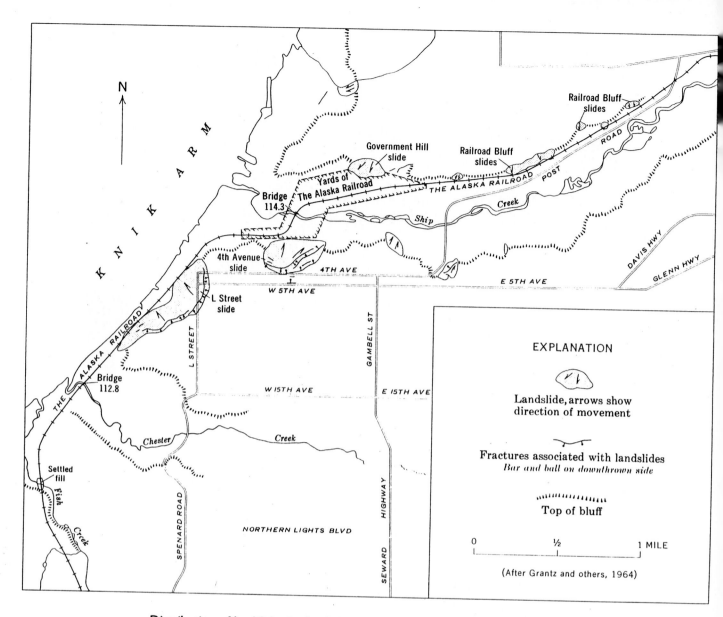

N

KNIK ARM

Railroad Bluff
slides

Government Hill
slide

Railroad Bluff
slides

Yards of
The Alaska Railroad

Bridge
114.3

THE ALASKA RAILROAD

THE ALASKA RAILROAD POST ROAD

Ship   Creek

DAVIS HWY

GLENN HWY

4th Avenue
slide

4TH AVE

E 5TH AVE

W 5TH AVE

L Street
slide

THE ALASKA RAILROAD

GAMBELL ST

EXPLANATION

Landslide, arrows show
direction of movement

Bridge
112.8

L STREET

W 15TH AVE

E 15TH AVE

Fractures associated with landslides
Bar and ball on downthrown side

Chester   Creek

Top of bluff

Settled
fill

SPENARD ROAD

SEWARD HIGHWAY

NORTHERN LIGHTS BLVD

0   ½   1 MILE

Fish Creek

(After Grantz and others, 1964)

Distribution of landslides in the Anchorage area and settled fill on Fish Creek. USGS

The Government Hill slide caused severe dislocations in the south-facing bluff on the north side of Ship Creek. Altogether, about 11 acres of land was involved, including about two and one quarter acres of bottomland below the bluff where the slide passed into an earthflow and spread out in the yards of The Alaska Railroad. The volume of earth involved was about 900,000 cubic yards. From flank to flank the slide had a width of 1,180 feet. From head to toe its greatest length, in the direction of slippage, was about 600 feet. The head of the slide regressed back about 400 feet behind the prequake bluff line, where it intersected the Government Hill Grade School. The slide devastated all but one wing of the school, destroyed two houses, damaged a third, left a fourth (since removed) perched precariously above a cliff, wrecked a shed in the railroad yards at the foot of the bluff, and did extensive damage to railroad equipment and trackage. If any good fortune accompanied the March 27 earthquake, it was timing; had school been in session, the disaster would have been unthinkable. The south wing of the school dropped as much as 20 feet vertically into a graben after being sheared cleanly in half. The east wing, also astride a graben, collapsed after being split longitudinally. The playground was a mass of chaotic blocks and open fissures.

The dramatic views of the Government Hill School show the extent of destruction.
COE

West High School

Anchorage's largest high school and the center for much of the city's higher education was totally destroyed. The $6,500,000 high school had been double-shifted with both high school and junior high students. In addition, it served as classroom space for the Anchorage Community College at night.

Heavy damage forced high school students to a double-shift program at East High School. Community events were cancelled due to the loss of the school's gymnasium and auditorium.

Other elementary and junior high schools received damage, and the Government Hill School was ruined. Supplies, books and school records were lost or strewn about in the schools.

Already hard-pressed for school buildings and supplies due to the rapidly growing community, the Anchorage Independent School District, had to come up with some quick emergency plans to house, feed and supply the hundreds of students left without their schools.

Damage was extensive at the West Anchorage High School, on the southside of Hillcrest Drive, just south of a bluff overlooking Chester Creek. Structurally separate parts of the school building reacted differently to the vibrations. The two-story classroom section was heavily damaged, especially the second floor. X-shaped cracks apeared on the outside walls. COE

This wooden-framed house was astride a fracture line in the L Street graben area at Eighth Avenue and N Street. USGS

A tree trunk split by a tension fracture in the Turnagain Heights lside area. Many trees were similarly damaged because their roots were firmly embedded in the frozen ground. USGS

The Anchorage International Airport control tower, a reinforced-concrete structure, collapsed, killing one occupant, injuring another and damaging the connecting walls of the adjacent terminal building. There terminal building was otherwise little damaged. At the airport post office building, a rear wall pulled away from the roof trusses and leaned outward; moderate nonstructural damage was sustained indoors. REEVE ALEUTIAN AIRWAYS

Sen. Ernest Gruening
looks into a store window
while on an inspection
trip to earthquake
damaged Anchorage. AMHA

Senator Gruening and Bob Bartlett
talk with presidential aide Edward
A. McDermott at the corner of
Fourth Avenue and C Street,
discussing the enormous damage
to downtown Anchorage. AMHA

The south side of Fourth Street
was cleared of destroyed buildings
and new buildings were erected.
COE

The photos on these two pages show the destruction caused by the Turnagain Heights slide, the largest, most complex and physiographically devastating landslide in the Anchorage area. It extended west to east along the bluff line about 8,500 feet. A total area of about 130 acres was completely devastated by displacements that broke the ground into countless deranged blocks, collapsed and tilted into odd angles. Seventy-five homes were destroyed. The ground surface within the slide area behind the prequake bluff line was lowered an average of about 35 feet. The volume of earth within the slide was about 12-1/2 million cubic yards. COE

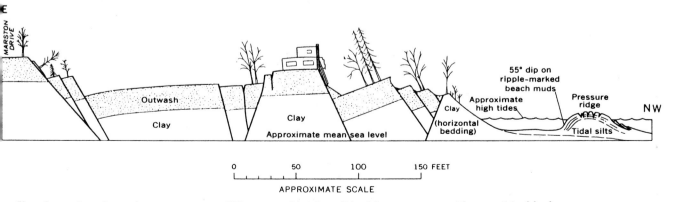

Sketch section through eastern part of Turnagain Heights slide. Note pressure ridge, upright blocks at center and to left of pressure ridge, and tilted collapsed blocks between. USGS

Lower end of C Street
and debris from the
Alaska Cold Storage Co.
ASL, U.S. ARMY COE COLLECTION, PCA
100-5

Heave in a street and the
destroyed Dalton and Co.
wholesale hardware. ASL,
U.S.ARMY COE COLLECTION, PCA 100-6

Sharp-crested pressure
ridge at Second and C
streets. A light pole was
uprooted and part of the
chimney on the building in
the background was
toppled. ASL, U.S. ARMY COE
COLLECTION. PCA 100-183

Bob Reeve and the Earthquake*

About 4 p.m., March 27, 1964, I made my way up to the Petroleum Club on the 15th floor of the Westward Hotel. It was my 62nd birthday and I thought I would have a few with my friends to get in training for a big family party commemorating this anniversary. Little did I suspect the smashing roaring show that was to mark this occasion put on by Mother Earth that was to influence the course of my life for months to come.

One cup led to another. It was a great day! We were great fellows, great oil men and great pilots and we believed in the brotherhood of man and yea, we could do no wrong!

At 5:35, I checked my watch and decided I had time for one more. As, Cliff, the bartender gave it to me there came an ominous tremor. At 5:36, it struck with brute force, with a roar and bang that could only be associated with a major upheaval from the bowels of the earth.

In a split second I found myself flat on my back and the south wall of the Club slammed over 30 feet and clobbered me on my head. It passed through my mind, "What the hell did that bartender put in that last drink!"

Simultaneously with my meditation, I felt a resounding crack a few inches from my head. An Ancient well drilling tool displayed on the wall tore lose and 100 lbs. of iron just grazed my medulla oblongata.

Then all hell really turned lose. Fifty tables, 150 chairs and hundreds of items of glassware, dishes, silverware, bottles, glasses, all the paraphernalia of a first class eating and carousing club, with the roar of the mill-tools of hell, in one big ball of furniture and bottles enveloped me in their embrace and from one end of the Club to the other I was tossed without mercy at the whim of the largest known disturbance of nature ever known or experienced in the Western Hemisphere.

I thought to myself—this roof can't possibly stand another shock like the last one. But each successive shock came with a monstrous cadence stronger than ever. I thought to myself—I have flown in every country in South, Central and North America and I expected to get killed some day in an airplane, but now my time was really up

Bob Reeve, in dark glasses, at the Petroleum Club on his birthday, March 27, 1964.

BOB REEVE COLLECTION

and what a hell of a way to die! I couldn't help remember the advice we always gave scared passengers in the old days of barnstorming, "You never get yours until your time comes."

Actually, I believe I was quite detached during the whole holocaust. My watch became unclipped from a button in my vest. I couldn't have accomplished this myself without considerable effort. I saw this watch on the floor. I thought, "That looks like my old Elgin," and it was. I stuck it in my pocket as I rolled with the punches.

About 5:40, it stopped. Except for the falling plaster and the last tinkle of the silverware and glasses, deathly silence prevailed. The lights were all out. I hied to the cloak room and found my coat but my hat took more doing.

In the dark I was conspicuous by my loneliness, when suddenly out of the haze of the dust and falling plaster, came a young fellow I recognized as Ken Yates. We were all alone. All my other fair weather friends had taken off and deserted me.

Bit by bit we made our way down the fire escape forcing open the jammed steel fire doors in every floor. About the third or fourth floor I began to get "my wind up" to a moderate degree. I had lost all track of the floors and believed I was descending into a bottomless pit into the bowels of the earth. At an estimated 40 minutes from the end of the quake we emerged into sunlight on Third Avenue.

Across the street was one of my friends. I said, "Where the hell did you disappear to?" He answered, "Bob, I just went for help."

He then asked me, "Were you scared?" "No," I answered, "But I passed three fellows on the way down who were really scared!"

It is reported the City Council is going to request me to leave town next March 27.

I think I will go to Washington, D.C. That is the headquarters of the Friendly (Federal) Aviation Agency!

* Bob Reeve was a famous bush pilot who started his flying career in Alaska in Valdez in the 1930s. After World War Two he founded Reeve Aleutian Airways which still serves the Aleutian Islands. The airlines museum office is located on 5th Avenue in downtown Anchorage.

Earthquake Picture Story Told On Inside Pages

EXTRA **Anchorage Daily Times** EXTRA

49TH YEAR ANCHORAGE, ALASKA, SUNDAY, MARCH 29, 1964 PRICE 10 CENTS IN ANCHORAGE AND VICINITY

CITY RALLIES FROM QUAKE

☆ ☆

SHOCKWAVE ONE OF MIGHTIEST

OFFICIAL CASUALTY LIST AS OF 2 P.M.

Seven persons were reported known dead in Anchorage and three seriously injured according to an earthquake casualty list compiled this morning.

However, no figures were available on the number of persons missing in city areas.

Thirteen persons who are missing were listed by city Civil Defense Headquarters. Anyone having information on any of those listed as missing were asked to call City Civil Defense.

Those listed as missing are:

Ruebel Grow, male, age 60, last seen going into driveway at 2016 West Marston Drive.

Andrew J. Chikoyak, male, native, five feet, five inches, 130 pounds. Probably on Fourth Avenue at time of earthquake.

Louis Wagner, male, age 21, probably in Sand Lake vicinity and probably riding with party named Burrells.

Georgina Ondola, female, age 20, probably in area of Sixth Avenue.

Pfc. Daneil Bures, possibly in Mt. Alyeska area.

Pvt. Gramby, believed in Palmer area.

Pfc. Richard Barnes.

Pvt. Thomas Hood.

Pvt. Dennis Planing.

M. Sgt. Harold Lord.

Jessie Martin, daughter of Betty Martin.

Pfc. and Mrs. Richard D. Wilson.

Construction workers demolishing the J. C. Penney store are searching for three missing persons last seen in the store.

Prononuced dead on arrival at Providence Hospital—where all injured from the Anchorage area were taken—were: William G. Taylor, 45, 3729 McCain Road, a Federal Aviation Agency employe who was in the control tower at International Airport; Mrs. Virgil E. Knight, 2114 Marston Drive; a baby about one year old, identified as the daughter of Mr. and Mrs. Jerry Ware, of Whittier, and a man identified only as J. J. Martinez.

Other victims taken directly to mortuaries were: Mary Louise Rustigan, wife of Baxter Rustigan, operator of City Cold Storage who lives on Peck Avenue; Lee Styer, 19, son of Mr and Mrs. Leroy Styer, 2800 Columbia Way, and a man identified only as Clayton Baker, who was picked up at 3339 Iliamna St.

Only eight persons, of a total of 108 brought to Providence Hospital for treatment, were admitted to the hospital and three of these are reported to be in serious condition.

Mrs. Jerry Ware of Whittier is in very serious condition with a crushed arm. Virgil Knight, husband of one of the dead victims, is in critical condition at the hospital.

Also seriously injured is a Mrs. Nona Oberbey, believed to have been in the Hillside Apartments on 16th Ave.

Providence is still caring for most of some 22 patients transferred from Presbyterian Hospital. There is no indication when the downtown hospital will be reopened.

The Air Force Hospital at Elmendorf was evacuated as a precautionary measure after the large masonry building was badly damaged by the quake. All patients were moved into bachelor officer quarters and hospital personnel quarters.

No fatalities were reported, however, and military authorities are now preparing a list of injured persons.

Only one natural death has been reported, that of Robert I. Smith, 36, of Talkeetna, brother of Theron Smith of Anchorage. His body is at Evergreen Memorial Chapel.

The bodies of quake victims Martinez, Taylor and Baker are at Anchorage Funeral Chapel. Mrs. Knight and the Ware child were taken to Angelus Mortuary. Mrs. Rustigan and Styer were taken to Angelus Mortuary.

Tonsina Due To Dock Here

Alaska Steamship Company's vanship Tonsina is scheduled to arrive in Anchorage Tuesday and unload at the city port.

The vessel—on its first trip as a vanship — had been originally scheduled to dock at Seward but was diverted directly to Anchorage after Friday's earthquake.

The Army Engineers Alaska District let a contract on an emergency basis this morning to Miller Bros. and the contractor started work repairing land approaches to the city dock so the ship can be unloaded.

A possible hazard—leaking gasoline from storage tanks — was apparently solved. The Air Force foamed the area and trucks have hauled in gravel and blotted the soaked area with sand.

The Engineers were also probing navigation approaches to the city port to see if there had been any changes in channels due to earthquake.

Men Flee Penney's Store As Quake Shatters W all

The World Was In A Weird Frenzy

Atwood Sees Home Torn Apart By Quake

(Editor and publisher Robert B. Atwood of the Anchorage Daily Times watched his home torn apart in the twisting, tearing movements of Anchorage's disastrous earthquake Friday night. The home was located on Marston Drive in Turnagain, overlooking Knik Arm. Here is his story.)

By ROBERT B. ATWOOD
The Anchorage Daily Times

Mrs. Atwood was leaving for the grocery store when I arrived home from the office about 5:30 Friday evening. I thought of going with her.

Then, I decided to stay home and practice on my trumpet while the house was empty. I could blow loud without disturbing anyone.

I had just started precisely that when the earthquake started. Earthquakes of the minor sort are not uncommom here but they always prompt me to stop what I am doing and watch what happens.

In a few short moments it was obvious that this earthquake was no minor one. The chandelier made from a ship's wheel swayed too much. Things were falling that have never fallen before.

I headed for the door, carrying my trumpet. At the door I saw walls weaving. This was no place for me. Out onto the driveway I went.

I was still carrying my trumpet.

On the driveway I turned and watched my house squirm and groan, as though in last mortal agony. It was as though someone had engaged it in a gigantic taffy pull, stretching it, shrinking it and twisting it.

I was glad my wife was not there to watch. She had designed it, planned it, built it with herself as architect, contractor and superintendent.

I became aware of the falling of tall trees in our yard and I moved to a spot where I thought I would be safe. But, as I moved, I saw cracks appear in the earth. Pieces of ground in jigsaw puzzle shapes moved up and down, tilted at all angles.

I tried to move away, but more appeared in every direction.

I was moving toward my neighbor's house, but I noticed that my house was moving away from me, fast. My neighbor's house was not standing still. All the world was in a wierd frenzy.

As I started to climb the fence to my neighbor's yard, the fence disappeared.

Trees were falling in crazy patterns with staccato crackling. Deep chasms opened up. Table top pieces of earth moved upward to stand like toadstools with great overhangs. Some turned at crazy angles.

A chasm opened beneath me. I tumbled down. It seemed to be an endless fall. Soft sand cushioned the impact. I was quickly on the verge of being buried. I was only one of many bits of debris tumbling into that chasm.

I found I couldn't pull my right arm from the sand. It was buried to the shoulder. Most of the rest of my body was also covered. I let go of my trumpet and my arm pulled free easily.

Somehow, even in that perilous position, I felt keenly the loss. I felt I had just lost my last contact with many things associated with a happy home.

Many thoughts flashed through my mind, but never did I think this was the end for me. I scrambled to stay atop the debris.

I ducked pieces of trees, fence posts, mail boxes and other odds and ends.

Then, I had the awful experience of watching my neighbor's home slowly collapse and slide into the chasm. For a time it threatened to come down on top of me, but the earth was still moving and the chasm opened to receive the house.

I feared for the life of my neighbors.

When the earth movement stopped, I climbed to the top of the wall of my chasm. I found angular landscape in every direction.

I found my neighbor, Warren Hines, carrying his young daughter.

We found his wife atop one of the high mushroom-like promotories. She was standing alone with her auto, marooned.

She said she had stopped outside of the gate of her home and watched the earthquake consume everything. We also found their son. Fate was kind to the Hines.

We climbed up and down chasm walls and under dangerous overhanging pieces of frozen ground to safety.

The children seemed to know we were in deep trouble. They responded marvelously. Never a whimper.

Helicopters were overhead but they couldn't land near us. The ground was too topsy turvy. After what seemed to be endless time, rescuers came to us and helped the party out of the quagmire that had once been a home.

Loss Estimated By Governor At $250 Million

In the incredible aftermath of one of the world's mightiest earthquakes, the people of Anchorage began to rebuild today on a hazy, quiet Easter Sunday.

The survey of damages and loss continued in the largest city of Alaska and throughout the coastal regions of the 49th State devastated by the giant quake which ripped the earth about 5:36 p.m. on Good Friday.

Anchorage counted seven confirmed fatalities early this afternoon and three serious injured—and an untold number of missing. Across the state and down the Pacific Coast, where giant tidal waves battered the shorelines, the death toll mounted—perhaps as high as 80.

Gov. William A. Egan, in Anchorage to direct state assistance, called the quake "the worst disaster Alaska has ever suffered."

"There is nothing to compare with it," the governor said.

"But the people do not consider this a beating or themselves licked," Egan said.

The governor said the Anchorage area suffered a total loss of at least $250 million. He called the figure conservative.

Hard hats and helmets were the Easter parade headgear attire as the big cleanup task got under way.

Anchorage Mayor George Sharrock, on duty almost continuously since the earth trembled with a mignty roar, expressed the confidence of the city as it looks ahead.

"I haven't found anyone who isn't going to rebuild," the mayor said. "It'll be better than before."

Anchorage and Alaska were not alone as the recovery operation began.

At his vacation ranch in Texas, President Johnson was up most of the night receiving reports of the disaster.

He greeted a news conference this morning as a weary-eyed, concerned national leader. He said he had no plans to visit Alaska. Federal orders already have been issued under the President's direction, declaring the quake zone as a disaster area.

Federal officials were quickly on the scene to assess losses and begin setting up procedures on what specific aid could be offered.

Alaka's two United States senators, E. L. Bartlett and Ernest Gruening, were among the first of the Washington officials to arrive.

In the immediate wake of the earthquake, hundreds of homes were shattered.

The Turnagain and West Turnagain areas were devastated along the bluff line overlooking Knik Arm.

Homes fell away as the earth sloughed off. Trees tumbled, cars fell into yawning pits. Mothers sheltered children in churning hallways of homes. Others led youngsters to safety.

The quake slipped buildings, shattered windows, sent grocery and merchandise flying in stores through the city.

Government Hill School split open. West High School was turned into a shambles. The new Four Seasons Apartment building, nearing completion just off L Street, collapsed.

The 14-story Mt. McKinley and 1200 I Street apartment buildings, Anchorage's highest buildings, were twisted and made uninhabitable.

The quake struck with shuddering force just as many offices were closing for the day, and many shops and stores were in the last half hour of the Friday pre-Easter business day.

The grinding force of the wrenching earth tore streets and lawns apart.

The ground heaved and structures buckled.

A thousand personal tragedies unfolded with the opening earth. Without panic, stunned people paused as they became aware of the awful might of what was happening.

J. C. Penney Co.'s five-story, year-old building on Fifth Avenue heaved and buckled. A dozen or more people stood with shock as the walls of Penney's sheared away, crushing half a dozen cars parked at the curb.

One of the first victims of the tragedy died in her car as the walls tumbled.

Across the city, the quake brought the normal life of a great city to a halt—and focused all activity into personal and community efforts to save lives.

The city mustered quickly, with the aid of untold hundreds of personal sacrifices playing a part in a stirring civic performance.

There was severe damage to the Cordova Building,

(Continued to Page 2)

The first Anchorage newspaper after the quake appeared on Sunday, March 29, two days after the disaster. AMHA

VALDEZ

This street fissure became a stop sign for this car. VA

Valdez

Valdez is the northernmost all-weather port in Alaska. Unlike Seward and Whittier, which are also all-weather ports, it is not a railhead but is connected with Fairbanks and the interior by highway. The town is on Port Valdez, the northeasternmost extension of Prince William Sound.

All port facilities were destroyed by the earthquake. A gigantic submarine slide off the face of the delta on which Valdez is built was the most disastrous event—it completely destroyed all docks and superstructures. Waves, ground cracks, shaking, and fire left all other port facilities and the seaward part of the town in ruins.

Shortly after the earthquake, the Corps of Engineers built a temporary dock on the newly formed waterfront, primarily for offloading of supplies needed in rehabilitation of the town but also to permit the small commercial and sport-fishing industries to resume work. Meanwhile, the likelihood of further submarine slides and continued settlement along the waterfront, and the danger of flooding by the Valdez glacier stream that built the delta, led geologists to advise complete abandonment of Valdez. This advice was followed by town officials who decided to build a new town at Mineral Point, about four miles by road west of the devastated community. The new site is far less likely than the old to be damaged by future earthquakes, and the modern docks and ferry slip that allowed Valdez to resume its place among Alaskan ports are founded on bedrock that is not susceptible to underwater slides.

The old townsite of Valdez in the background and the new townsite in the foreground. ASL, U.S. ARMY CORPS
ENGINEERS, PCA 100-225

Valdez's downtown area
like its waterfront was
total destruction. VA & COE

There wasn't much left of the Seward waterfront or the Texaco tank farm. COE & UAA, WALTER BENESCH COLLECTION #72-152-93N (VF)

Military personnel stand in front of the Switzerland Inn with its sign on the ground. UAA, WALTER BENESCH COLLECTION #72-152-235N(VF)

The 37 victims of the earthquake in Valdez. COE

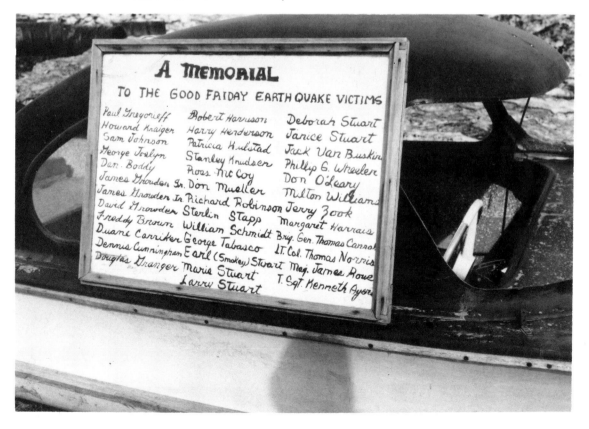

Two foot in diameter spruce trees snapped off by a local wave at elevations between 88 and 101 feet above the low water mark at Shoup Bay in Port Valdez. USGS

McKinley Avenue on April 4, 1964, has been cleaned up but many of the stores are propped or boarded up. COE

WHITTIER

This dramatic and well-publicized photo shows the force of the seismic wave. A two by six plank was driven through a 10-ply tire at Whittier. USGS

Whittier is at the head of Passage Canal on the northeast side of the Kenai Peninsula in southcentral Alaska about 50 miles southeast of Anchorage and 40 miles southwest of the epicenter of the earthquake. Passage Canal, a west-southwest-trending fiord, is a western arm of Prince William Sound and is about 11 miles long and one and a half miles in average width.

The main port facilities of Whittier are on the south shore of Passage Canal about one mile east of its western end. The town is built on a fan-shaped delta formed by Whittier Creek—a creek fed by Whittier Glacier. The delta has a maximum width of approximately two miles, is about one and a half miles long, and rises from sea level to an altitude of 90 feet with a fairly uniform slope of 60 feet per mile.

The port of Whittier was constructed under the supervision of the Corps of Engineers in 1942-43 to provide an all-weather terminal for The Alaska Railroad. During World War II, Whittier and Seward served as the two all-weather railroad ports that safe-guarded the flow of military supplies, equipment and personnel from tidewater to Anchorage and Fairbanks.

Whittier was hard hit by the earthquake and 13 persons were lost. At the time, only 70 people were living at Whittier. The official 1960 census listed a population of 800; however, this figure included military personnel who were subsequently transferred when the Army closed its Whittier operation. Only one body was recovered; the remaining 12 persons were presumed dead. In addition, the earthquake destroyed or made inoperable a major part of the port facilities. Total damage to the Federally and privately owned facilities at Whittier was in excess of $5 million.

The loss of the Whittier port facilities, coupled with destruction of those at both Seward and Valdez left Alaska without any all-weather port for unloading supplies for movement either by rail or highway to the metropolitan areas of Anchorage and Fairbanks.

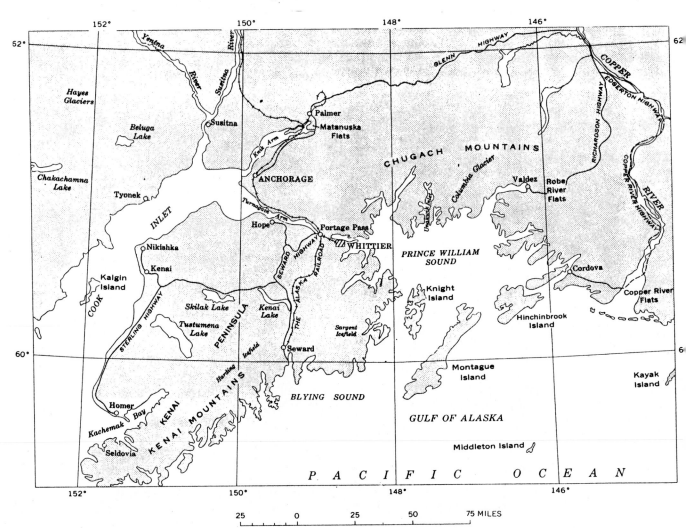

The destroyed fuel-storage tanks at the Whittier waterfront. COE

Destroyed building at Whittier, possibly part of Columbia Lumber Company. COE

Remains of the railroad facilities at Whittier. ASL,

U.S. ARMY COE, PCA 100-232

An aerial view, looking north, of the remains of the Columbia Lumber Company at Whittier. Homes of the workers were also destroyed. Twelve of the 13 people lost in the seismic wave were associated with the lumber company. USA

The freighter *SS Chena* bottomed out three or four times in Valdez during the wave action. It is shown here docked at Whittier after the quake. COE

PORTAGE/GIRDWOOD

Portage under water in May 1964. Once it became evident to local residents that the town would be flooded continually during extreme high tides, they moved many of the buildings to higher ground—some to Indian, about 20 miles northwest of Portage, on the Seward-Anchorage Highway. COE

Portage/Girdwood and Vicinity

Portage

The small town of Portage, about 40 miles southwest of the epicenter, is on the Seward-Anchorage Highway at the head of Turnagain Arm. The town is on a flat surface underlain by fine-grained silt, sand and gravel. Locally, the water table is within a foot and generally not more than three feet from the surface.

Seismic motion at Portage was northwest-southeast and lasted for five and a half to six minutes. As in other localities, the motion started gently, but at Portage it became violent within a few seconds after it started. Vibration caused structural damage to several buildings in town and generated numerous cracks or fissures in the ground. George Larson, of Portage, reported that during seismic shaking the chimney at a gasoline station was destroyed; one-half of it fell into the building and the other half fell outside. Seismic motion damaged most of the buildings in town. In addition, ground fissures that formed beneath the buildings during the earthquake caused further damage. The largest of the fissures was four feet wide; their average width was only two feet.

Although seismic shaking and resultant ground fissures damaged buildings, the highway, and the Alaska Railroad grade, the subsidence had the most damaging effect. The Portage area had a regional subsidence of slightly more than five feet and, in addition, local subsidence of one and a half to two feet. Local subsidence was greatest in areas underlain by thick fill, such as the highway roadbed which, in places, subsides more than three and a half feet.

Once it became evident to local residents that the town would be flooded continually during extremely high tides, they moved many of the buildings to higher ground—some were move to Indian, about 20 miles northwest of Portage, on the Seward-Anchorage Highway.

Girdwood

The small town of Girdwood, about 55 miles west-southwest of the epicenter of the earthquake, is on a gently sloping alluvial fan where Glacier Creek flows into Turnagain Arm. The town is bordered on the east, west and north by mountains, and on the south by Turnagain Arm.

The Portage liquor store. Notice the silt deposited on the ground by the high tides. COE

Seismic motion at Girdwood was northwest-southeast and lasted for about four to five minutes. One person who was driving a car on the Seward-Anchorage Highway at Girdwood reported that the motion was so violent that he could not control his vehicle. When one of his passengers got out of the car she was thrown to the ground.

Many fissures developed on the lower lying areas underlain by the finer grained deposits. Water and mud were ejected from some of the fissures. Reports on homes and other structures in Girdwood are scarce, but those obtained indicate that seismic shaking did not directly damage any structure. However, seismic shaking did generate numerous fissures throughout the town. Locally, some slight displacement down-slope occurred in the water-soaked fine-grained unconsolidated sediments. Damage was widespread on the railroad grade and highway roadbed.

Five feet of regional subsidence and an additional three feet of local subsidence occurred at Girdwood. This total eight-foot subsidence was enough to put much of the lower lying areas of the town under water during high tides. During the high tides of April 14, 1964, all of the highway, much of the railroad west of the railroad depot, and all of the town between the railroad and highway were submerged. Water was as much as three feet deep in some of the buildings, and subsequently the buildings were moved to higher ground or placed on stilts.

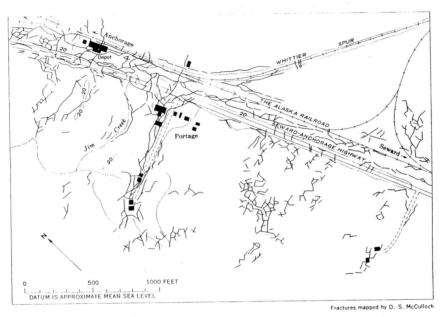

Fractures mapped by D. S. McCulloch

Major earthquake-induced fissures in Portage area. The entire area shown was inundated by high tides on April 14, 1964. USGS

Road damage on the Seward-Anchorage Highway at Portage. AMHA, US ARMY PHOTO B70-15-72

A collapsed highway bridge at Girdwood. A bailey bridge has been built over it to open up the highway again. AMHA, U.S. ARMY COE, B80·27·13

The military was called out to sandbag areas in the Girdwood area that were being inundated by tidal waters. A sign for the new Mt. Alyeska ski resort is in the background. AMHA, U.S. ARMY CORPS OF ENGINEERS #B80·27·12

On Aug. 10, 1964, Portage, on the Seward—Anchorage Highway experienced a 28-foot tide due to the regional subsidence caused by the Good Friday earthquake. USGS

SEWARD

The fishing boat, *Regent*, was beached several hundred feet inland from the head of Resurrection Bay. COE

Seward was one of the cities most heavily damaged by the earthquake. The city is near the head of Resurrection Bay, on the southeast coast of the Kenai Peninsula, and about 75 airline miles south of Anchorage. The climate is mild and humid because of the influence of the Gulf of Alaska. Seward is one of the few ports in south-central Alaska that is ice free the entire year. It therefore provides year-round access from the coast by railroad and highway to Anchorage and the interior of Alaska.

Before the earthquakes of March, 27, 1964, the economy of Seward was based mostly on shipping. Freighters, barges, tankers, and fishing boats docked regularly in the harbor. Most of the freight was transhipped to other communities by road or rail. Texaco, Inc., and the Standard Oil Co., of California had established large tank farms on the waterfront. Fishing boats unloaded their catch, and at least one cannery was in operation.

The entire economic base of the town was wiped out by the near-total destruction of harbor facilities during the earthquake. Damage was caused chiefly by shoreline and offshore landsliding and by locally generated waves, seismic sea waves, and fire. A tectonic downdrop of approximately three and a half feet caused formerly dry low areas to be covered by water at high tide.

Strong ground motion at Seward, which was in a north-south direction at least part of the time, lasted three to four minutes. Nearly all accounts indicate that the shaking started gently but increased markedly in a few seconds and continued to grow in violence until people could hardly stand without support. Reportedly the ground rose and fell like waves, trees bent in unison, and buildings swayed back and forth. Two gantry cranes at The Alaska Railroad dock bounded off their tracks and into Resurrection Bay, and automobiles rocked from side to side. Several chimneys fell, windows were broken, and foundations were cracked in various parts of the city. The Seward city hall was damaged beyond repair by shaking, but the building is said to have been in poor condition before the earthquake. Some other public buildings were damaged to some extent by shaking. Material on shelves tumbled to the floor, and glassware breakage, in such places as bars and liquor stores, was heavy. Water and sewer lines were ruptured in several parts of the city and in Forest Acres subdivision.

As the shaking started, rocks began falling from

Downtown Seward before the quake. UAA

some of the steeper valley walls. As shaking continued, rock slides were triggered in Jap Creek canyon and Box Creek canyon. Snow avalanched down the walls of Lowell Creek canyon and of several tributary valleys.

The more extensive and spectacular effects of the earthquake, however, were along the Seward waterfront. Between 30 and 45 seconds after violent shaking began, the distal part of the Seward fan, an area extending from the Standard Oil Co., dock to beyond the San Juan dock, began sliding seaward as a result of large-scale offshore landsliding. Slice after slice of ground along the shore slid progressively as shaking continued, until a strip of harbor area 50-500 feet wide had disappeared into the bay. Large fractures broke the ground surface behind the slide area and extended several hundred feet inland as shaking continued. Some fractures near the Texaco tanks reportedly opened and closed repeatedly during the shaking; some were at least 20 feet deep. They filled quickly with water and, as the shaking continued, spewed muddy water at intervals.

A pre-quake view of Seward, built on an alluvial fan-delta near the head of Resurrection Bay on the southeast coast of the Kenai Peninsula. UAA

The fishing fleet was hit hard by the seismic wave, as it was in Kodiak. COE

Damage caused by seismic waves to the old Alaska Railroad dock and facilities. COE

The Seward Community
Library suffered severe
damage from the wave.
UAA #72-152-94N

Tank farm on fire. AMHA, B.
HULM PHOTO

More than 86 houses
were destroyed by the
wave. USS #72-152-72N

An aerial view of the northern part of the Seward waterfront showing the destroyed Texaco tanks and the railroad tracks (bottom right) that dropped into the bay. A, B, C and D streets run approximately perpendicular from the left side of the photo towards the sea. The limit of fractured ground is on the left side of the photo. UAA #72-152-93N

The Texaco Inc. tanks on the northern part of the Seward waterfront were heavily damaged; several were destroyed by fire. COE

The old Alaska Railroad dock and facilities were partially dropped into the bay. This photo was taken sometime after the quake as the dock has been repaired. COE

-48-

The Alaska Railroad facilities in Seward were mostly destroyed by the quake and tsunami wave. Track was destroyed, twisted or dropped into the bay, buildings were flattened and engines and rolling stock were overturned and smashed. COE

A 79-ton Diesel switch engine was thrown 125 feet from its tracks. USA, SC613417

The seismic wave picked up this truck and wrapped it around this tree. AMHA

The tank farms on fire along the waterfront. AMHA 504

An aerial view of Seward after the quake. The Standard Oil Co. dock, Army dock, and San Juan dock are gone along with most of the Alaska Railroad facilities. A lot of the downtown area also has disappeared.
AMHA, U.S. ARMY CORPS OF ENGINEERS B80-27-2

A portion of Seward was cleaned up sometime after the quake. Many holes appeared in sections of town with the removal of destroyed buildings and equipment. AMHA, USA PHOTO #B79-38-30

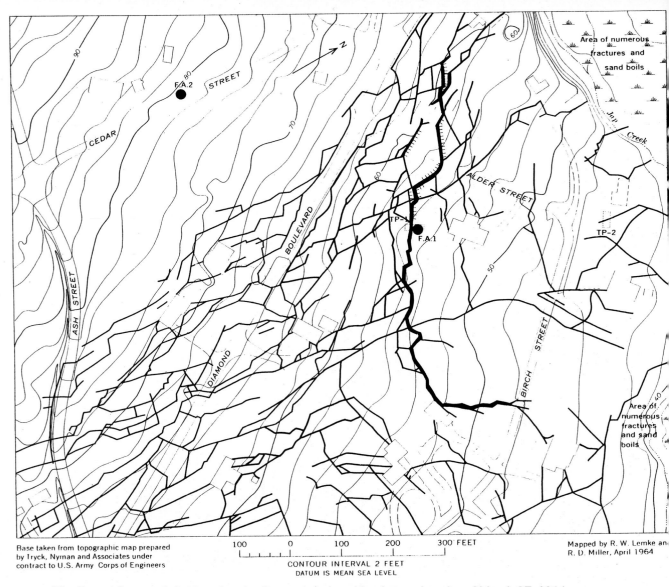

Base taken from topographic map prepared
by Tryck, Nyman and Associates under
contract to U.S. Army Corps of Engineers

100   0   100   200   300 FEET

CONTOUR INTERVAL 2 FEET
DATUM IS MEAN SEA LEVEL

Mapped by R. W. Lemke and
R. D. Miller, April 1964

The Forest Acres subdivision showing fractures induced by the earthquake of March 27, 1964. USGS

**One of numerous ground
fractures in the Forest
Acres subdivision north of
Seward. This fracture was
about two feet wide.** USGS

VIA R.D. MILLER

KODIAK ISLAND

The business district of Kodiak. GP

Kodiak

The town of Kodiak is on the northeast coast of Kodiak Island at latitude 57°47'30" N. and longitude 152°24' W. The downtown area is at the head of Inner Anchorage, a northeast extension of St. Paul Harbor. Kodiak is sheltered from Chiniak Bay and the Gulf of Alaska by several islands east of the town. The major protective islands are Long Island, Woody Island and Near Island.

The quake was felt in every community on Kodiak and the nearby islands. It took the lives of 18 people in the area by drowning; this includes two in Kodiak and three at Kaguyak. Property damage and loss of income to the communities is estimated at more than $45 million.

The largest community, Kodiak, had the greatest loss from the earthquake. Damage was caused chiefly by 5.6 feet of tectonic subsidence and a train of 10 seismic sea waves that inundated the low-lying areas of the town. The seismic sea waves destroyed all but one of the docking facilities and more than 215 structures; many other structures were severely damaged. The waves struck the town during the evening hours of March 27 and early morning hours of March 28. They moved from the southwest and northeast and reached their maximum height of 29-30 feet above the mean lower low water at Shahafka Cove between 11:00 and 11:45 p.m., March 27. The violently destructive seismic waves not only severely damaged homes, shops and naval station structures, but also temporarily crippled the fishing industry in Kodiak by destroying the processing plants and most of the fishing vessels. The waves scoured out 10 feet of sediments in the channel between Kodiak Island and Near Island and exposed bedrock. This bedrock presented a major post-earthquake construction problem because no sediments remained into which piles could be driven for foundations of waterfront facilities.

Because of tectonic subsidence, high tides now flood Mission and Potatopatch lakes which, before the earthquake, had not been subject to tidal action. The subsidence also accelerated erosion of the unconsolidated sediments along the shoreline in the city of Kodiak.

Seismic shaking lasted four and one half to five and one half minutes at Kodiak and had a rolling motion. Inasmuch as most of Kodiak is underlain by bedrock or by only a thin veneer of unconsolidated sediments, very little if any damage occurred from ground motion or seismic shaking. The ground motion, however, did cause a massive short circuit and power failure.

Estimates of damage to public, private and commercial facilities of approximately $24,736,000, were reported. The waves destroyed more than 215 structures and left more than 600 people homeless out of a total population of 2,658.

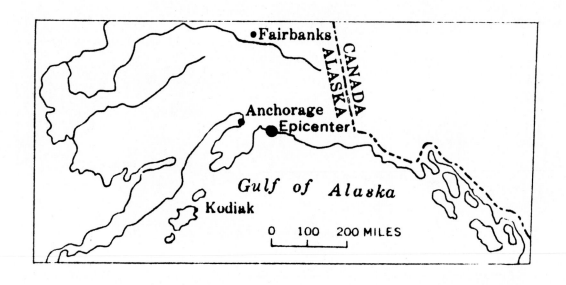

A pre-quake view of Kodiak. KHS

This whole area of Kodiak was wiped out by the seismic wave. KHS

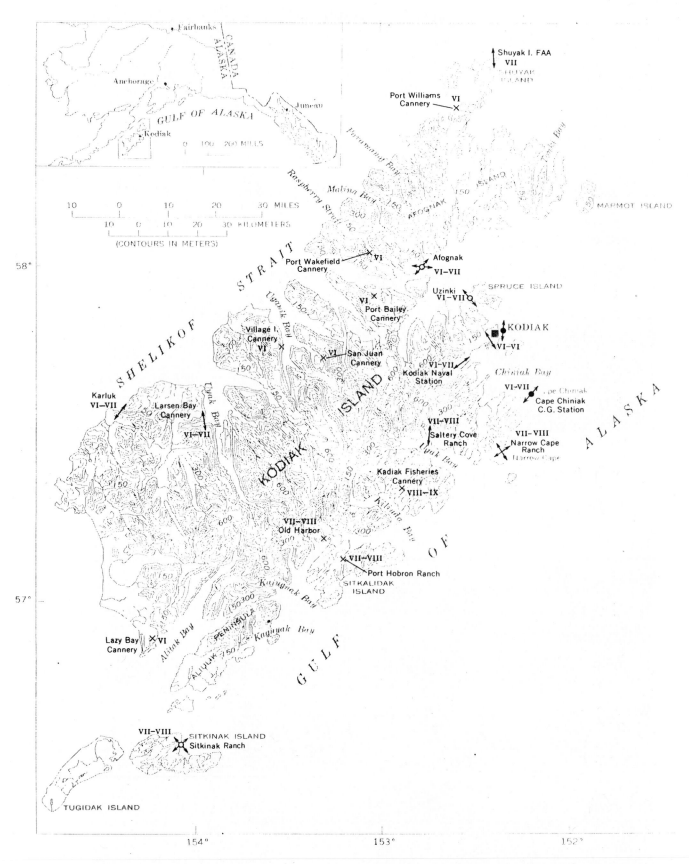

Reported ground motion, sounds, ground waves, and assigned Mercalli intensities on Kodiak and nearby islands. The directions of reported ground motion are shown by arrows; localities at which sound was reported are shown by solid circles, localities at which ground waves were reported by open circles, and assigned Mercalli intensities by Roman numerals. USGS

Small boat harbor

Alaska Packers Association

Small boat harbor

Alaska Packers Association

Aerial views of Kodiak, scale 1:6,000. The top view was taken on Sept. 10, 1962, the bottom view on April 14, 1964. Damage to the small boat harbor and the downtown area is very evident. USGS

Court Apartments

Telephone Company

BENSON AVENUE

REGANOFF AVE

Selief (boat)

School

Wave destruction in downtown Kodiak. View is looking west toward the intersection of Benson and Reganoff avenues. USGS VIA ALF MADSEN

The movie theater in downtown Kodiak. The movie playing at the time was "Heroes Die Young." KHS

These four scenes of downtown Kodiak show the force of the seismic wave that hit the town. More than 215 structures were destroyed along with dozens of fishing boats.

The Kodiak small-boat harbor before the quake (top) and afterwards (bottom). GP

Businesses in Kodiak before the quake (top) and remains (bottom). GP

Some of the small fishing boats beached by the seismic wave. GP

Kodiak business district destruction. GP

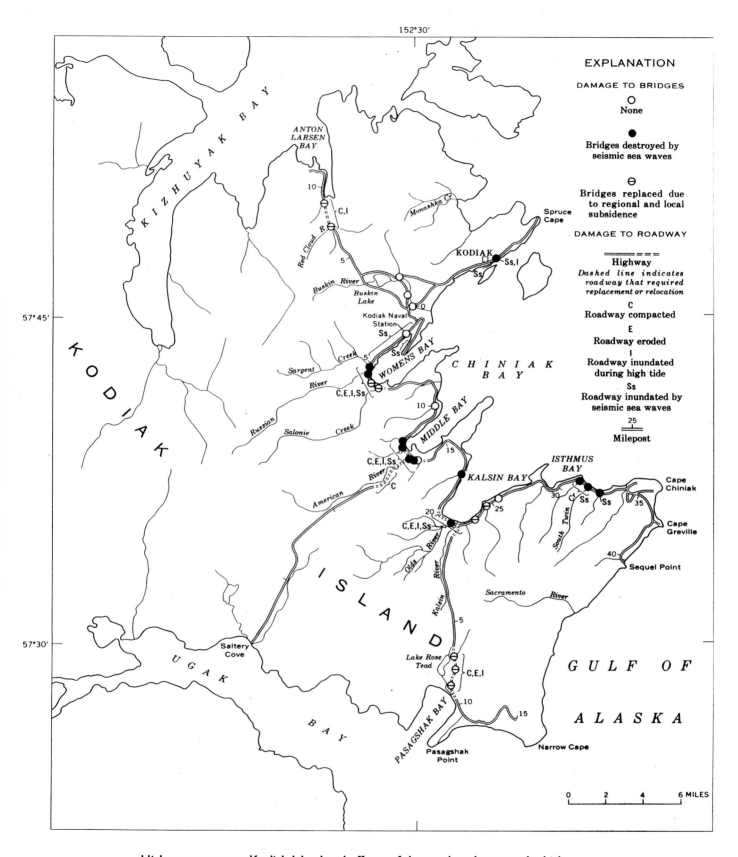

Highway routes on Kodiak Island and effects of the earthquake upon the highways. USGS

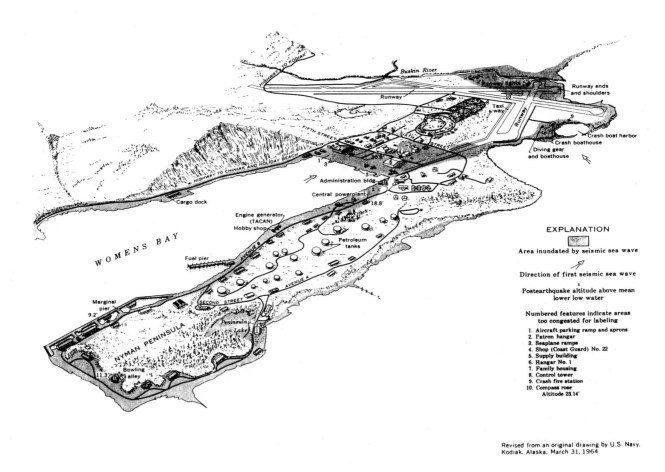

EXPLANATION

Area inundated by seismic sea wave

Direction of first seismic sea wave

x Postearthquake altitude above mean lower low water

Numbered features indicate areas too congested for labeling

1. Aircraft parking ramp and aprons
2. Patron hangar
3. Seaplane ramps
4. Shop (Coast Guard) No. 22
5. Supply building
6. Hangar No. 1
7. Family housing
8. Control tower
9. Crash fire station
10. Compass rose
    Altitude 23.14'

Revised from an original drawing by U.S. Navy.
Kodiak, Alaska, March 31, 1964

Area of maximum inundation by seismic sea waves and structures damaged at Kodiak Naval Station.

Kodiak Naval Station

The Kodiak Naval Station, five miles southwest of Kodiak, was severely damaged by the earthquake. The station was inundated by at least 10 seismic sea waves which reached a maximum height of 25 feet above post-earthquake mean lower low water between 11:16 and 11:34 p.m. on March 27, 1964. The first seismic sea wave that flooded the station did not do severe damage because it behaved much like a rapid rise of tide, but the subsequent and more violent waves destroyed most of the docking facilities and several other shoreline structure. The waves struck the station from the southwest and from the east.

The shoreline structures that were not destroyed required reconstruction because the 5.6 feet of tectonic subsidence put them under water during the highest tides. Furthermore, the subsidence accelerated erosion during high tide of the soft unconsolidated sediments and fill in the low-lying areas of the station.

Seismic shaking did little damage to the station housing facility, but it was responsible for compaction of sediments, lateral displacement of a seawall, and the development of fissures in the aircraft parking area. The ground motion was south-southeast—north-northwest to north-south in direction.

The Naval Station reported an unusual case of radioactive contamination. The inundating seismic sea waves entered a building in which radio-nuclides were stored. The contamination was restricted to the building only, however, and did not spread throughout the station.

Interior of the Navy
Exchange at the Kodiak
Naval Station. U.S. NAVY

Damage to the naval
station's hangar. UAA, WALTER
BENESCH COLLECTION #72-152-
225N(VF)

Seaplane ramp along the
shore of Womens Bay
showing approximate
high-water level reached
by the first seismic wave
USGS

The Kodiak Fisheries Cannery remains in Shearwater Bay along the north shore of Kiliuda Bay on Kodiak Island. Cannery buildings in the foreground were split during the quake and the seaward parts were washed away by the waves. The timber foundations can be seen on the beach and in the water. The barge to the right was moved in to replace the destroyed facility. USGS

Part of the village of Afognak showing some of the eroded road along the water, new beach berms (outlined by dashed lines) and part of large lagoon ponded behind beach berm. USGS

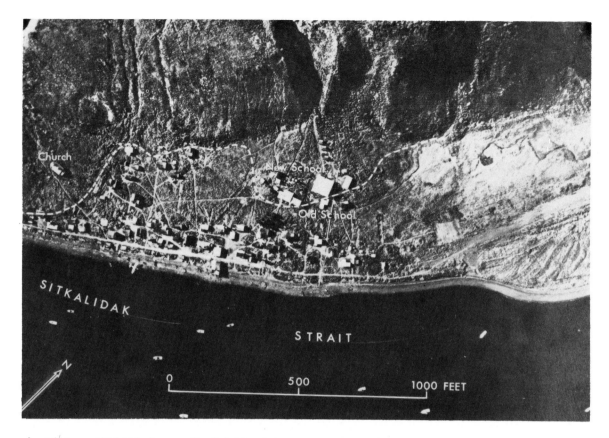

Aerial view of Old Harbor on Kodiak Island showing the approximate inland limit of inundation by the sea wave (dashed line). USGS

Citizens of Old Harbor in front of the school, on the edge of the high water mark of the seismic sea wave. UAA, WALTER BENESCH COLLECTION #72-152-50N (VF)

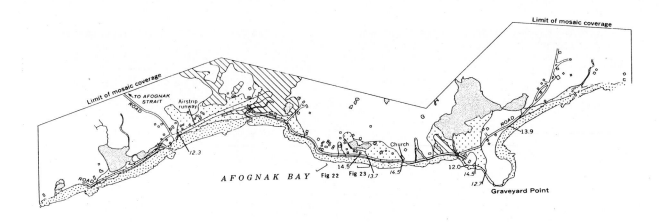

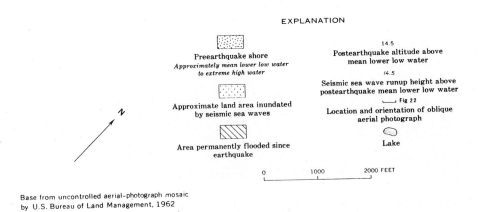

EXPLANATION

Preearthquake shore
*Approximately mean lower low water
to extreme high water*

14.5
Postearthquake altitude above
mean lower low water

Approximate land area inundated
by seismic sea waves

14.5
Seismic sea wave runup height above
postearthquake mean lower low water

Fig 22
Location and orientation of oblique
aerial photograph

Area permanently flooded since
earthquake

Lake

0   1000   2000 FEET

Base from uncontrolled aerial-photograph mosaic
by U.S. Bureau of Land Management, 1962

**Planimetric sketch map of Afognak showing approximate limits of inundation by seismic sea waves and
the areas flooded by ponding behind barrier beaches.**

Afognak

Afognak was abandoned because of the extensive damage incurred from tectonic subsidence and seismic sea waves. The seismic effects, estimated Mercalli intensity VI–VII, did not directly cause any significant property damage at Afognak. Serious long-term damage, however, resulted from tectonic subsidence estimated to be from three and one-half to five and one-half feet. The subsidence has resulted in rapid erosion of the coast, landward shift and building up of beach berms to the new higher sea levels, and flooding of extensive low-lying areas behind the barrier beaches. Inundation of low-lying parts of the village by a train of seismic sea waves having maximum heights of 10.8 feet above postearthquake tide level (14.5 feet above post-earthquake mean lower low water) caused losses of about half a million dollars to homes, vehicles, bridges and personal possessions.

The subsidence forced the village to be relocated to a site just south of the original village on the north end of Kodiak Island. It was named Port Lions because of the help from the Lions clubs across the United States and cost approximately $816,000.

OTHER COMMUNITIES

Seldovia as it appeared a year after the quake. The inner harbor facilities and breakwaters have been restored and the piers and docks have been raised to compensate for the three and one-half foot tectonic subsidence. USA

Seldovia is an important fishing and cannery center on Seldovia Bay, one of the few ice-free harbors along Cook Inlet, 16 miles southwest of Homer. Most of the business buildings and docks were strung out along a mile-long boardwalk that skirts the harbor area. Virtually all the damage was caused by tectonic subsidence of about three and one-half feet. In contrast to that at many communities on the Kenai Lowland, the shaking at Seldovia was felt for only about three minutes and was described by local residents as "mild" or "moderate;" it tippled a few small objects in stores and homes but caused no structural damage. The sea began to recede and fill erratically during the shaking, but seismic sea waves were not noticed until after 8:00 p.m., two and one-half hours after the quake. There were several more waves during the night, with the highest one of 26 feet, coming between 4:00 and 5:00 a.m. on March 28. One of the early waves carried away the floats of the small-boat harbor, and the highest wave inundated part of the boardwalk and damaged stock in a few store buildings. Long-term damage caused by subsidence was far greater than that caused by seismic sea waves. The boardwalk and all buildings along it became subject to flooding at high tides, as did one end of the airport runway. Breakwaters had to be raised four feet to protect the small-boat basin, the damaged floats had to be repaired, and the airport runway raised. Sandbags were used temporarily to protect the boardwalk, and the city dock was raised. Direct compensation costs for the effect of subsidence amounted to slightly more than $1 million. Later, an urban renewal plan was adopted to restore the entire waterfront by building an extensive dike and filling the land behind it to levels above the post-earthquake high tides. TOP: AMHA B79·38·5, MIDDLE: AHL, US ARMY COE, PCA 100-220, BOTTOM: COE

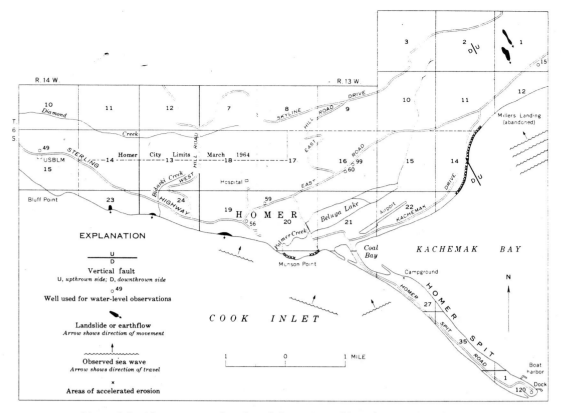

Map of the Homer area showing slide areas and beach erosion points. USGS

High tide at Homer on April 12, 1964, (A) Standard Oil Company tank farm in six feet of water. (B) Land's End Hotel raised on jacks. (C) Water rose high enough to flow through the windows of the Salty Dawg Saloon. (D) A new storm berm encroaching on the spit southwest of Land's End Hotel. USGS

The earthquake shook the Homer area for about three minutes. Land effects consisted of a two- to six-foot subsidence of the mainland and Homer Spit, one earthflow at the mouth of a canyon, several landslides on the Homer escarpment and along the sea bluffs, and minor fissuring of the ground, principally at the edges of bluffs and on Homer Spit. Hydrologic effects consisted of at least one and possibly two submarine landslides at the end of the spit, seiche waves in Kachemak Bay, ice breakage on Beluga Lake, sanding of wells, and a temporary loss of water in some wells. Seismic damage to the community was light in comparison with that of other communities closer to the epicenter. One submarine landslide, however, took out most of the harbor breakwater. The greatest damage was due to the subsidence of the spit, both tectonically (two to three feet) and by differential compaction or lateral spreading (an additional one to four feet). Higher tides flooded much of the spit. The harbor and dock had to be replaced, and buildings on the end of the spit had to be elevated.

The Land End Resort (top) had to be elevated above the high water line. The small boat harbor had to be moved into the spit itself as the former basin's breakwater had washed away. AMHA, B79-38-25 & ASL, U.S. ARMY COE, PCA 100-199

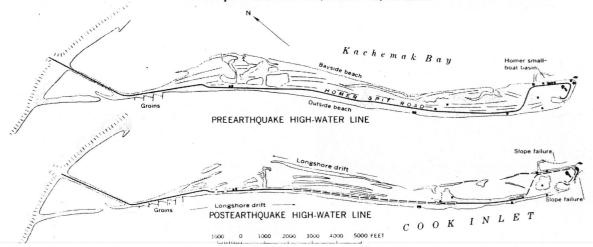

Comparison of the high-water line along Homer Spit before and after the earthquake and submergence of March 27, 1964. Light lines on Spit represent old beach burms. High-water line traced from U.S. Army Corps of Engineers aerial photographs, September 1959, and from U.S. Bureau of Land Management infrared photographs, August 1964. USGS

Cordova

Cordova is a fishing, canning and distribution center for much of the Prince William Sound region; earlier in its history it was the rail-ocean trans-shipment point for copper ore from the rich Kennecott mining district farther inland. Of all the communities affected by the earthquake, it stands out as the one where tectonic uplift did far more damage than seismic vibration and waves combined. The city is accessible only by air or water.

Despite heavy shaking, there was no structural damage in the city. Damage at the airport was caused entirely by fissures that intersected the foundation of the FAA control building, taxiways, and underground utilities. All bridges on the segment of the Copper River Highway between the city and the airport that cross unconsolidated deposits of the delta were destroyed or badly damaged, and the roadway itself settled differentially and was cut by fissures. The bridge spanning Eyak River which had foundations on bedrock was not damaged.

Reports differ as to the number and timing of the sea waves that struck Cordova. The first wave observed near Boswell Bay was a strong surge about 6 p.m. Many rapid but gentle rises and withdrawals, presumably due to passage of seismic sea waves, at Cordova and vicinity in the hours immediately after the cessation of shaking caused no damage. The highest wave, which almost coincided with the predicted high tide of 13 feet, struck the waterfront area at about 12:30 a.m. on the 28th. This wave, about 20 feet high, flooded the shore to a height of about 34 feet above post-earthquake mean lower low water, or about five feet above the extreme high-water level. All waves were calm, without breakers, but high water and swift currents during these and possibly even later waves did considerable damage to the port facilities and to moored boats. The deck of the city dock was lifted off its pilings and displaced; one cannery was damaged when a boat smashed against its piling. The waves also struck the low area toward Eyak Lake, where several small structures were washed away and a sawmill was destroyed. The city's radio tower, on the tidal flats, swayed violently with the shock waves, but remained intact until much later when it was struck and toppled by a floating structure. The waves also damaged the roadway and washed out a bridge at Hartney Bay on the road between Cordova and Point Whitshed.

Tectonic uplift raised the land surface in the vicinity of Cordova about six feet. This uplift was far more disastrous to all port facilities than were the earthquake vibrations or the seismic sea waves. One cannery at Crystal Falls, one the edge of the Copper River Delta about five miles south of Cordova, was abandoned because boats could no longer reach it. At Cordova, all dock facilities were raised so high that they could be reached by boats only at highest tides. Several nearby canneries had to extend their docks more than 100 feet to permit access. The area in the vicinity of the city dock and the small-boat basin was above water at most tides; an extensive and difficult dredging project, together with new breakwaters and dock repairs, was necessary to make the facilities usable. In the course of this work, which was done by the Corps of Engineers, the boat basin was much enlarged, and about 20 acres of new land, eventually usable for industrial purposes, was made from material dredged from the boat basin.

Damage to the port facilities was not the only adverse result of tectonic uplift. The Cordova fishing fleet normally uses Orca Inlet in its travel between town and the shallow fishing grounds off the Copper River Delta. Because uplift made the inlet waters too shallow for even small boats, laden vessels had to wait for extremely high tides or take the much longer and more hazardous route through Hinchinbrook Entrance and through Orca Bay. Because neither solution was economically practicable, it was necessary for the Corps of Engineers to dredge a new channel through almost the entire length of Orca Inlet. The total cost of dredging, port facilities, and repairs to the town's uplifted sewer outfall was about $3 million, but part of this cost was offset by enlargement of the small-boat basin over its pre-earthquake capacity and by development of new industrial land.

Cordova as it appeared after the quake. Tectonic uplift left docks inaccessible to ships except at very high tides. Reconstruction involved dredging of the harbor and rebuilding the docks and small boat basin. ASL,

U.S. ARMY COE, PCA 100-187

Wave-damaged structures at Port Nellie Juan, site of an inoperative cannery on the northeast shore of McClure Bay. A wave, which ran up to the snow trimline along the shore, damaged these buildings and drowned the three caretakers of the cannery. usgs

This barge, 60 feet long by 25 feet wide, broke loose from its moorings by a violent local wave in Port Nellie Juan. It was turned upside down, and deposited among the trees 200 feet from the shoreline at about 30 feet above mean lower low water. usgs

Vertical displacement in the Kenai Lowland, an area from Kasilof on the east shore of Cook Inlet to Chickaloon Bay on the south shore of Turnagain Arm. A scarp more than 200 feet long and two to three feet high was produced in a thick section of frozen peat and organic silt. USGS

Wildwood Station, an Air Force base five miles north of Kenai, experienced severe damage from the quake. Seven hundred personnel were stationed there at the time. An elevated steel water tower holding 145,000 gallons collapsed and the rush of released water struck the adjacent officer's club injuring one man. During the quake the tank began to sway. About halfway through, the manhole cover at the top blew off and water spouted out. The tower then split in two pieces and failed; one half fell against the petroleum-oil-lubricants building southwest of the tower center and the other half fell to the northwest. USGS

Aerial view of the Chenega native village site at the southern end of Cheneya Island on Knight Island Passage in western Prince William Sound. The arrows indicate the approximate limits of the seismic wave. Twenty-three of the 75 inhabitants were lost. The survivors were resettled at Tatilek. USGS

The Cheneya village site. The schoolhouse remained standing but all but one of the houses (pilings remain) were swept away. USGS

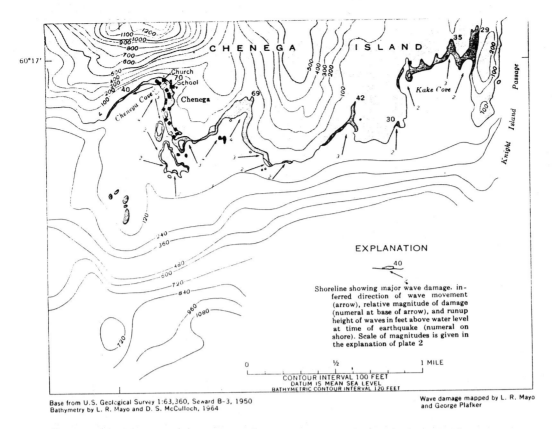

Distribution and intensity of wave damage at Chenega and vicinity, Chenega Island. USGS

The Latouche waterfront, a large abandoned mining camp on the northwest shore of Latouche Island. Local waves destroyed all the docks and piers along the shore and demolished or damaged many of the waterfront buildings. Waves as high as 58 feet hit the shore along Latouche Passage and the ground, in places, raised 11 feet putting the former port above the reach of most tides. USGS

Several large rockslides occurred on glaciers in the Gulf of Alaska area, east of the earthquake's epicenter. This is a pre-earthquake view of Sherman Glacier taken in August 1963. USGS

This view of Sherman Glacier was taken in August 1964 showing the rockslide. This slide was formed by the collapse of Shattered Peak in the middle distance. USGS

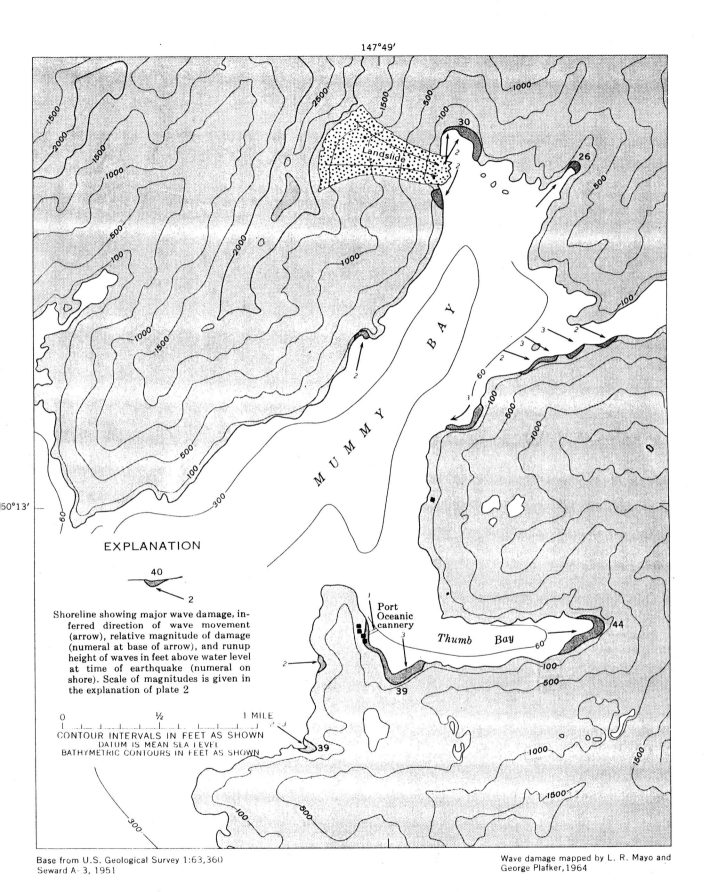

147°49'

30

26

Landslide

M U M M Y   B A Y

EXPLANATION

40

2

Shoreline showing major wave damage, in-
ferred direction of wave movement
(arrow), relative magnitude of damage
(numeral at base of arrow), and runup
height of waves in feet above water level
at time of earthquake (numeral on
shore). Scale of magnitudes is given in
the explanation of plate 2

0   ½   1 MILE

CONTOUR INTERVALS IN FEET AS SHOWN
DATUM IS MEAN SEA LEVEL
BATHYMETRIC CONTOURS IN FEET AS SHOWN

Port
Oceanic
cannery

Thumb   Bay

44

39

39

60°13'

Base from U.S. Geological Survey 1:63,360
Seward A-3, 1951

Wave damage mapped by L. R. Mayo and
George Plafker, 1964

**Distribution and intensity of wave damage in the vicinity of Port Oceanic cannery
at Thumb Bay, Knight Island.** USGS

Montague Island is the most southerly of three long narrow islands that trend northeast across the south side of Prince William Sound. The island is 51 miles long and four to 12 miles wide. It has a rugged topography with dense growths of timber and brush on most of the valley floors. Two reverse faults on the southwestern area of the island were reactivated during the earthquake. New fault scarps, fissures, cracks and flexures appeared in bedrock and unconsolidated surficial deposits along or near the fault traces. Significant subsidence occurred along the shoreline and landslides were evident along the fault scarps. The only two known surface faults produced by the earthquake occurred on this island. COE

ROADS AND BRIDGES

The Kenai Lake Bridge in July
1964. COE

The great earthquake that struck Alaska at about 5:36 p.m., Alaska standard time, Friday, March 27, 1964 (03:36:13.0 Greenwich mean time, March 28, 1964) severely crippled the highway system in the south-central part of the State. This part of Alaska has approximately 60 percent of the total population and produces more than 55 percent of the State's gross product and revenue. Thus, the disastrous effects of the earthquake upon the highway system materially affected the economy of the whole State. After the seismic shaking and attendant seismic sea waves had stopped, much of the highway system lay in ruins. Roadways were fractured or were blocked by avalanches; many had sunk out of sight or had been washed away. Most of the bridges were damaged and many were completely destroyed. Some of the destroyed bridges lay in the creeks and rivers they once spanned; others had been washed away.

This destruction isolated communities on the Kenai Peninsula from Anchorage and the rest of the State. On Kodiak Island, Chiniak was isolated from the town of Kodiak.

In south-central Alaska there were, at the time of the earthquake, 830 miles of primary and secondary roads with 204 bridges. Approximately 186 miles of roadway and 141 bridges were damaged; 88 of the 186 miles was severely damaged. Ninety-two bridges required replacement. Total damage amounted to about $46,798,292.

The Alaska Department of Highways responded quickly to the emergency, and by early summer of 1964 all damaged routes were passable. The only section of road not reopened by the fall of 1966 was the Copper River Highway between the Copper River (mile 27.1) and the Million Dollar Bridge (mile 49.0).

A close-up view of Number 4 span and a horizontal fracture in the pier of the Million Dollar Bridge. This view is looking northeast. USGS

The Million Dollar Bridge on the Copper River Highway. Number 4 span off of Number 4 Pier. This view is looking southwest. USGS

Contact between steel
truss and concrete deck
on Pier 26, Copper River
Bridge at Mile 27.1,
Copper River Highway.
USGS

The Turnagain Arm slide
in May 1964 was still
covered with snow. Seven
avalanches occurred from
just west of Girdwood to
Portage along the highway
and railroad. COE

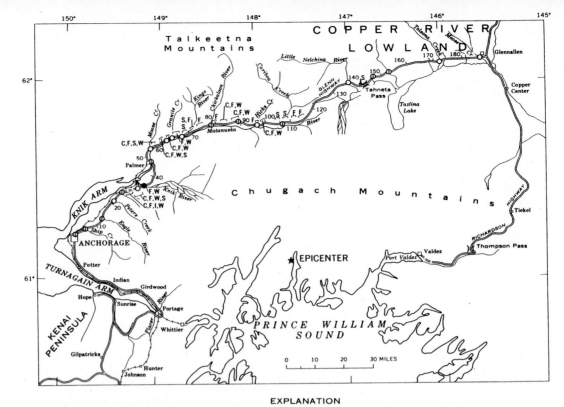

Route of Glenn Highway and the effects of the earthquake upon the roadway. USGS

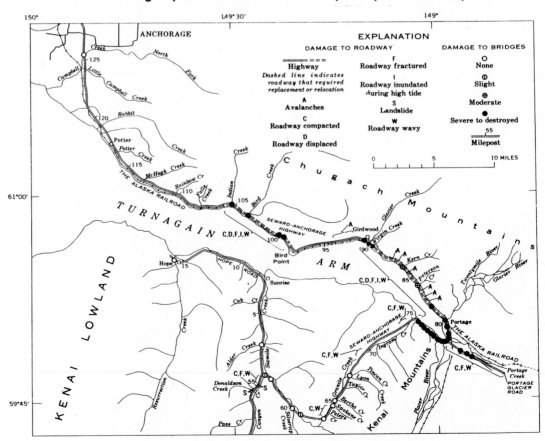

Routes of part of the Seward-Anchorage Highway, the Hope Road and the Portage Glacier Road, and the effects of the earthquake upon them. USGS

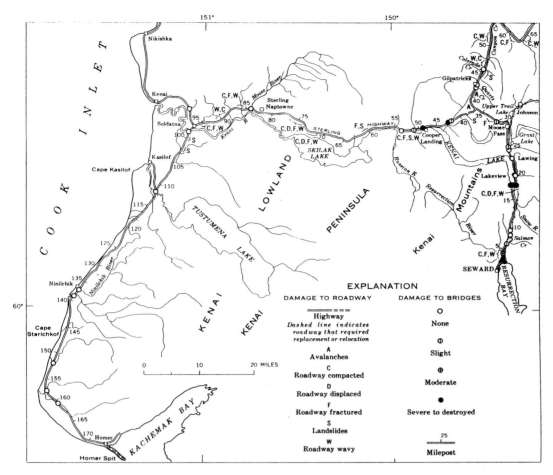

Routes of Sterling Highway and part of Seward-Anchorage Highway, and effects of the earthquake upon them. USGS

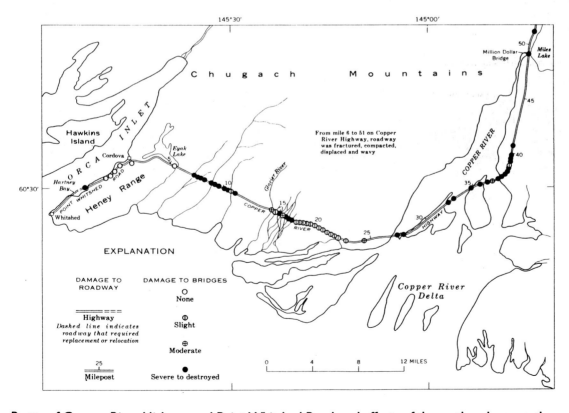

Route of Copper River Highway and Point Whitshed Road, and effects of the earthquake upon them. USGS

The Twentymile River railroad and highway bridges at Portage. All of the concrete deck sections of the highway bridge except one were knocked from their piles, and some piles were driven through the concrete. The railroad bridge was compressed and some of its piers shifted. USFS

Major damage occurred near mile 58.5 of the Copper River Highway. Complex fractures with relatively large lateral and vertical displacements, produced by movement of saturated fine sand and silt can be seen. The Allen River, which drains Allen Glacier is in the background. USGS

Vertical displacement of the Seward-Anchorage Highway, southwest of Ingram Creek. The pavement in the foreground is underlain by sediment; in the background, by bedrock. The shovel is 19 inches high. USGS VIA HELEN FOSTER

A good example of highway destruction common throughout the road network of south-central Alaska. COE

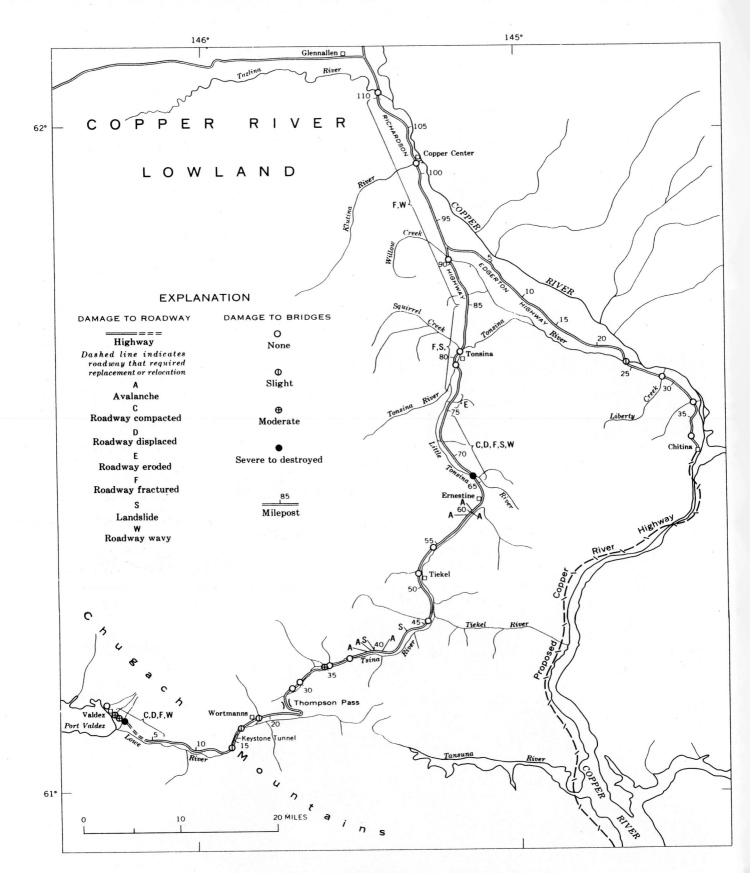

Routes of the Edgerton Highway and part of the Richardson Highway, and effects of the earthquake on the highways. USGS

MILITARY OPERATIONS

The Alaska National Guard, both army and air, was called into action immediately and provided much needed help to Anchorage and isolated communities throughout the affected areas. This guard stands over a fissure in the Turnagain housing area in Anchorage. UAA, WALTER BENESCH COLLECTION, 72-152-2N (VF)

As communications were re-established between military installations and State and City Civil Defense Headquarters and among the various other devastated communities of south central Alaska calls for aid and assistance began pouring into the Command Post of the Alaskan Command. Those in the adjacent Greater Anchorage area were able to receive almost immediate attention. Due to a combination of bad weather and lack of runway information and navigational aids, those requiring airlift support could not be reached until morning.

At dawn, the first of some 17 Provider (C-123) transports of Elmendorf's 5017th Operations Squadron roared down the runway with relief supplies and equipment for such earthquake and tidal wave ravaged communities as Seward, Valdez and Kodiak.

Alaskan Air Command alerted the Air Force Logistics Command to respond to Alaskan Command requirements immediately.

Military Air Transport Service and Air Force transport aircraft from strategic locations throughout the United States were alerted for use in expediting emergency care in Alaska.

During the next 21 days, this transportation was to develop into the most massive airlift of its type ever recorded by the U.S. Air Force. Over 3,700,000 pounds of cargo were airlifted and distributed to hard-hit areas.

Military Air Transport Service broke its own disaster relief cargo hauling record by moving more than 2,750,000 pounds of supplies in support of HELPING HAND. This involved more than 1,300 hours of flying time.

Utilized in the vast Military Air Transport Service airlift were some 55 giant Globemasters (C-124s), two huge Cargomasters (C-133s), four Stratolifters (C-135s), two Super Constellations (C-121s) and one Liftmaster (C-118). Supplementing these were eight Stratofreighters (C-97s) from the Military Air Transport Service's reserve fleet in the western states Air National Guard units which brought in approximately 195,000 pounds of cargo.

Foodstuffs, supplies and equipment comprised most of the cargo which ranged from baby food to massive construction equipment. Also transported were some 500 passengers which included three Stratolifter (C-135) trips to air-evacuate 58 patients from USAF Hospital, Elmendorf, to Travis Air Force Base, California.

In the two weeks following the disaster, U.S. Army Alaska light aircraft flew 589 hours on 556 sorties in disaster relief, carrying 137,075 pounds of cargo and 947 passengers. Most of this lift was by Army Shawnee (CH-21) helicopters and Otter (UIA) fixed-wing craft, but a total of 66 Army aircraft of seven types, assigned to the U.S. Army Alaska Aviation Battalion were included in the effort.

Known support figures for the first 12 days following the initial disaster reveal that Alaskan Air Command Providers (C-123s), Skymasters (C-54s), Workhorse (H-21) helicopters, plus Beaver (U-6A) propeller and Tee Bird (T-33) jet liaison aircraft of the 5017th Operations Squadron, and the 317th Fighter Interceptor Squadron, flew more than 200 hours on almost 200 sorties airlifting 560,300 pounds of cargo and approximately 850 passengers and evacuees.

Alaska Air National Guard Providers (C-123Js) of the 144th Air Transport Squadron from Kulis Air National Guard Base, flew nearly 160 hours handling approximately 315,000 pounds of cargo and more than 150 passengers.

Perhaps the most outstanding single operation of all the Air Force airlift support was a combined Military Air Transport Service—Alaskan Air Command—Alaska National Guard mission. It involved the airlifting of a Bailey Bridge from Elmendorf Air Force Base to the Soldotna-Kenai area on the Kenai Peninsula for the Army Engineers. This bridge was to replace one knocked out by the earthquake at Cooper's Landing on the lower end of Kenai Lake.

A female resident of Portage is assisted from an Air Force H-21 helicopter at Elmendorf Air Force Base during the evacuation of the small destroyed town. USAF

The Alaskan Air Command, U.S. Air Force, was activated to provide personnel and equipment for quake relief. Additional equipment and personnel were flown in from the lower 48 and even Hawaii. UAA, WALTER BENESCH COLLECTION, 72-152-226N (VF) AND 72-152-61N (VF)

The Elmendorf Base Exchange sustained considerable damage. UAA, WALTER BENESCH COLLECTION #72-152-59N (VF)

Emergency hospital facilities were set up in the parking lot and in bachelor non-commissioned officer's quarters at the Elmendorf hospital. The quarters saw duty as an emergency clinic, wards and operating rooms, while the parking lot was the site of the dining hall, water lines, power systems and quarters. USAF

A mobile control tower from Tinker Air Force Base in Oklahoma was airlifted to Elmendorf Air Force Base within 36 hours of the quake, which knocked out the base control tower. The tower was fully deployed and operational when it arrived at Anchorage. USAF

The Elmendorf MATS Terminal sustained considerable damage. A cast concrete chimney toppled off its foundation and punctured the roof. USAF

Bluff Road at Elmendorf Air Force Base slipped down from the ground movement. USAF

Guardsmen slept wherever they could after providing much needed service to quake victims.
UAA, WALTER BENESCH COLLECTION, 72-152-36N (VF)

The U.S. Army in Alaska was also pressed into service to provide relief.
COE

THE ALASKA RAILROAD

The Alaska Railroad took the full force of the earthquake from Seward north beyond Anchorage.
COE

Within two hours of the first earthquake tremor, the federally owned Alaska Railroad had sustained more than $35 million worth of damage. The destructive agents took many forms. Seismic sea waves, landslides, and waves generated by slides from the edges of deltas destroyed or severely damaged costly port facilities at Seward and Whittier—ports through which passed most of Alaska's waterborne freight. The damage was compounded by seismic shaking, ground cracking, and burning fuel carried inland by the waves (Grantz and others, 1964; Kachadoorian, 1965; Lemke, 1967). More than 100 miles of roadbed settled or was displaced and broken by ground cracks in areas underlain by unconsolidated sediments. In the same areas, 125 bridges and more than 110 culverts were damaged or destroyed. Landslides overran or carried away several miles of roadbed and destroyed or severely damaged buildings and utilities. Other railroad structures were destroyed or damaged by seismic shaking. Tectonic subsidence lowered the land as much as five and a half feet along the railline and made about 35 miles along the shore susceptible to flooding at high tide and to accelerated marine erosion.

The southern terminus of The Alaska Railroad is the deepwater all-weather port of Seward, built on a fan delta in Resurrection Bay fiord on the Gulf of Alaska. North from Seward (mile 0) the rail line runs about 64 miles across the steep and rugged glaciated terrain of Kenai Peninsula to Portage, where it is joined by a 12-mile spur line to a second deepwater all-weather port at Whittier, on Prince William Sound. From Portage to Anchorage the rail line is built along the north shore of Turnagain Arm at the foot of steep mountains; at Potter it swings inland over gently rolling plains of glacial deposits to the main rail yards in Anchorage, mile 114, on the shore of Cook Inlet. Leaving Anchorage, the line continues across the glacial plain along the southeast side of Knik Arm to the wide flood plain of the Knik and Matanuska rivers that empty into the head of the arm at about mile 146. At Matanuska, on the northern edge of the flood plain, the line is joined by a 22-mile spur that follows the northwest side of the Matanuska River to Palmer, Sutton, Jonesville and Eska. The main line turns west at Matanuska, then swings north in a long curve along the valley of the Susitna River which it follows through the mountainous terrain near Denali National Park. Crossing the drainage divide of the Alaska Range at Summit (mile 312.5) the rail line continues north in the Nenana River valley to the town of Nenana at mile 411.7. From here it swings to the northeast and reaches Fairbanks at mile 470.3.

Tension on the Rockey Creek railroad bridge was relieved by shearing the bolts in an angle bar and pulling the track apart. USGS

Rails were literally pulled from their ties and bent by the force of the earthquake. COE

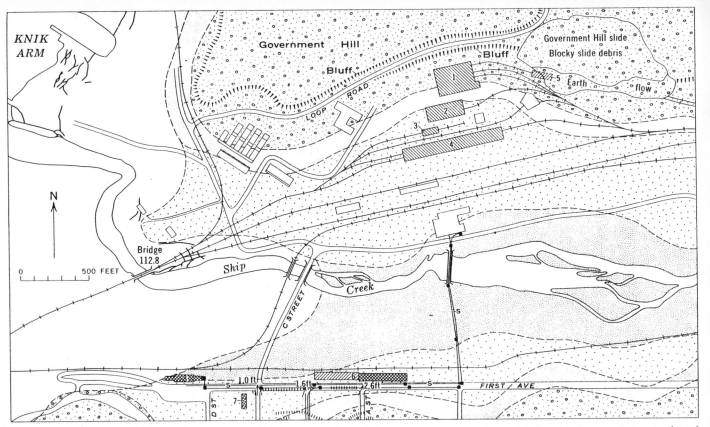

Base by J. Morrison, The Alaska Railroad,
and postearthquake aerial photographs

Geology after Miller and Dobrovolny (1959)

EXPLANATION

Modern estuarine sediments

Flood-plain deposits

Terrace and glacial-outwash gravel

Outwash sand and gravel

Bootlegger Cove Clay

– – – – – –
Approximate contact

'''''''''
Pressure ridges at the
toe of 4th Avenue
slide (Hansen, 1965)

2.6ft ←
Direction and amount of
horizontal displacement
of benchmarks (Shann
and Wilson, Inc., 196

Ground cracks

DAMAGED RAILROAD STRUCTURES

1 Heavy Equipment-Diesel Repair
2 General Repair Shop
3 Wheel Shop-Mechanical Offices
4 Car and Coach Shop
5 On-track Storage. Butler Building
6 Freight Depot
7 Office Annex (Satellite Building)
8 Passenger Depot

Shaking

Slide

Building damage

Shaking and slide

Utilidors

——s——
Steam and condensate

•—•—•—•
Electric and communications

**Map of the railroad
buildings and buried
utilities, surficial geology,
and landslide features in
the Anchorage railroad
yards in Ship Creek valley.**
USGS

**Alaska Railroad yard
damaged by earthflow
from Government Hill.**
USGS

About 4,000 feet of the Alaska Railroad bed along Potter Hill, two and one-half miles north of Potter gave way causing major damage. ALASKA RAILROAD

The railroad depot at Portage was heavily damaged. AUTHOR'S COLLECTION

The Whittier barge slip after the earthquake with one tower remaining. AUTHOR'S COLLECTION

The Whittier barge slip two weeks before the earthquake. Freight cars were brought up by barge from the west coast and off-loaded to Alaska Railroad tracks for the trip to the mainline. AUTHOR'S COLLECTION

The barge slip was rebuilt after the quake. AUTHOR'S COLLECTION

The Union oil tanks burning at Whittier. AUTHOR'S COLLECTION

The wave destroyed the waiting room of the Whittier Alaska Railroad Depot. COE

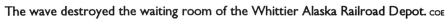

Destroyed tanks at Seward. COE

The railroad took a real beating at Seward from the seismic wave. USA

Railroad rails shifted back and forth laterally due to compression of the railway embankment. COE

CRESCENT CITY AND THE WEST COAST

Texaco tank farm on fire on Highway 101 South near Elk Creek. DNHS WALT HARRIS COLLECTION

The Crescent City disaster exceeded all prior combined effects in historical time from tsunamis on the United States West Coast. Damage estimates ranged from $11 million to $16 million.

These estimates substantially increased the earlier estimate of $7.4 million made shortly after the disaster. In Crescent City there were 10 fatalities due to drowning. In the early hours of the disaster, 12 people were hospitalized and 12 others were treated as outpatients. These numbers probably do not reflect the injuries sustained in the clean up. The port facilities and 29 city blocks containing 172 businesses, 12 house trailers and 91 homes were damaged or destroyed. The businesses and homes on Highway 101 South were particularly hard hit and eight of the fatalities occurred there. Twenty-one boats were sunk, due in part to their being moored at both ends. The Coast Guard cutter *Cape Carter*, a lumber tug and a few fishing boats managed to escape the harbor and ride out the waves in the open sea.

A tsunami advisory bulletin was issued at 9:30 p.m., PST, by the Seismic Sea Wave Warning System in Honolulu and was followed by a warning at 10:37 p.m. These warnings gave an estimated arrival time of midnight. Since the system does not attempt to predict the wave heights, there was nothing special about the warning to distinguish it from the many alerts that had resulted in harmless waves. Low lying areas were being warned when the first wave arrived at 11:39 p.m., just after high tide.

The first rise exceeded the gage limit but was estimated to have been 14 feet above mean lower low water (MLLW), or about nine feet above the tide level. The wave period was about 29 minutes and it flooded the lower parts of town to 2nd Street. The second wave was smaller, at six feet above tide beginning about 12:10 a.m.

Believing the worst was over as had always been the case in the past, many merchants and sightseers converged on the area having been alerted by television, radio and friends. Officials attempted to limit access to the area by sightseers to prevent looting, but businesspersons and residents were allowed to pass.

The third wave also exceeded the limits of the gage which failed altogether at this time. It was estimated to have been 16 feet above MLLW. It was at least a foot over Citizens Dock. A fire started at

Nichols Pontiac and houses on the lower end of town floated off their foundations. The draw down after the third wave was exceptional. The curator at the Battery Point Lighthouse reported that it receded 0.75 of a mile beyond the end of the outer breakwater. Boats were left on their sides in the mud.

Most of the damage and fatalities were caused by the fourth and largest wave beginning about 1:40 a.m., and peaking about 2:00 a.m. It reached a height of 20.78 feet above MLLW or about 15.7 feet above the expected tide. There is some confusion in the various accounts on the timing and wave count. The beginning wave arrival times given here are basically from the rise above the expected tide from the tide gage record. Most popular accounts refer to times near the wave maximum. Some accounts missed the second wave, which was smaller, and treated the largest wave as the third wave.

The third and particularly the fourth waves picked up logs, cars, trucks and other debris which acted as battering rams against buildings. One log penetrated the Post Office. The mail was sucked out but later most of it was painstakingly recovered. Fallen electrical wires posed additional hazards and at least one person was burned by contact with the wires while in the water.

Many people were at high risk: swimming for their lives; wading in deep and swift flowing water; floating on car and trailer tops; standing on furniture and on roof tops in flooded homes, motels, and businesses; and floating in moving homes and cars. Ten drowned—a relatively small number considering the large number of people in the water or in dangerous situations. Many people were helped to safety by use of heavy equipment such as road graders and log loaders.

The retreating waves left a huge amount of debris behind: timbers, 2.5 million board feet of lumber, perhaps 1,000 automobiles, shattered buildings, silt, and fish from the bay. Fish were found everywhere: in hanging flower baskets, rafters, desk drawers, in walls, and in large piles. Sand was not notably left behind as tsunamis have strong draw back currents which clean up such deposits. Telephone and electrical lines were destroyed. The harbor was silted up in places and needed dredging. Many of the old buildings were built of sturdy redwood timbers but floated from their foundations.

Daly's Department Store at 3rd and J streets had 18 inches of water from the third wave. DNHS WALT HARRIS COLLECTION

Many people were rescued by local authorities and ordinary citizens. Sgt. Donald McClure assisted S/Sgt. Stuart A. Harrington, both airmen stationed at a nearby radar station, as they were caught in the great tsunami on the Klamath River. McClure did not make it to shore. DNHS,- WALT HARRIS COLLECTION

Devastation was everywhere in the downtown area as a result of the four waves. This scene is looking down 2nd Street where it intersects with Highway 101. DNHS

Second Street the night of March 28 between waves. Magruder's had three to four feet of water hit the building along with many logs brought along with the successive waves. DNHS

Inside a store between 2nd and 3rd streets on I Street. A car had literally been washed into the store. DNHS

Tidal Wave Floods Crescent City, 7 Dead, Some Missing, 29 City Blocks Lie In Ruins!

Extreme Emergency Declared, Gov. Brown Arrives, Civilian Defense, Red Cross On Scene

CRESCENT CITY AMERICAN

SPECIAL EDITION   10c PER COPY   CRESCENT CITY, CALIFORNIA, SATURDAY, MARCH 28, 1964

Whipped into a fury by a savage Alaskan earthquake, a giant tidal wave rolled in from the Pacific under cover of darkness early this morning leaving in its wake a still undetermined number of dead at the time of this writing, and 29 business blocks in ruins.

The surges began rolling in at midnight; at first, with minor damage, but one recorded at 1 a.m. was higher, then at 1:40 came a destructive giant that gushed through the downtown section and on top of that, civilian defense officials said, came another that leveled some buildings, moved others and tossed cars and trucks around like so many matchsticks.

At 5 a.m., Civilian Defense Director William Parker, declared a state of extreme emergency. At 8 a.m. a joint meeting of the Del Norte county board of supervisors and the city council of Crescent City was held.

An hour and a half later, at 9:30 a.m., Governor Edmund G. "Pat" Brown, who had spent the night in Humboldt county, arrived by plane for an on-the-spot inspection of the tragedy, and looking forward to such measures as the state may be able to take to help relieve the situation.

Penny Ebbutt, who, representing civilian defense, said business establishments destroyed or damaged by the wave are not covered by insurance against such disaster. Mrs. Ebbutt had worked throughout the night in the Del Norte sheriff's office, which served as disaster headquarters.

Other women working through the night included: Eleanor Parsons and Noreen Zander of the Del Norte sheriff's office, and Janice Yoeman of the Crescent City police department.

Civilian defense personnel, Sheriff O.E. Hovgaard and deputies of the sheriff's office; Chief Andrew Keyzers, Crescent City police and police reserves, National Guardsmen under command of Bernard McClendon, and scores of volunteer citizens joined in heroic efforts that kept the toll of human life far below what it otherwise would have been.

Local facilities for taking care of the homeless were set up in rapid fire order (this included many local people who opened their homes to those in need). Two men and a woman, Wally Reed, Mrs. McDonald, and Mr. Patreno, representing the National Red Cross, also arrived this morning.

Emergency facilities were set up at the Del Norte fairgrounds by Acting Welfare Director Gertrude McNamara, County Sanitarian Joe Creisler went into action to take measures for protecting health, and County Building Inspector Walter Davis began condemning unsafe buildings. Doctors and nurses at Seaside Hospital were out in full force, and the ambulances of both Wier's and Roeder's Mortuaries were in service.

Road Commissioner Harley Forkner and crew began the tough task of clearing log-jammed and debris strewn roadways.

Hit hardest were the business establishments throughout the southeast portion of the city. This included the Crescent City

LATE BULLETIN

Governor Edmund G. Brown declared Crescent City a disaster area, following an inspection trip this morning. As such, the city is entitled to all the benefits incident to such designation.

Seven people who lost their lives, had been identified at press time, according to Sheriff O.E. Hovgaard.

They are Mr. and Mrs. Earl Edwards, Mr. and Mrs. Wm. Clawson; "Frenchie" last name uncertain, but known locally as having been engaged in carpentry work; and two children, Bonita Ione Wrigt and William E. Wright.

Also passing away suddenly was Oran Magruder, widely known founder of Magruder's redwood mfg. and gift shop on Second Street. Although it was believed the cause was a heart attack, it was not thought the attack was associated with the tidal wave.

Postmaster Michael Neish said local mail is being received at the old building. "There was about five feet of water in the post office," Neish said, "but we expect to be back in by Monday."

Richard Lantz, manager of Wells Fargo's Crescent City branch bank, said today that the bank will open for business in temporary quarters at 388 H Street. Its present quarters are at Second and K Streets, one of the worst devastated areas of the city.

post office on Third Street, and some of the establishments as far north as Fourth Street.

The damage mounts into many millions of dollars. There were no reliable estimates at press time, and the full extent, which grows by the hour as crews look over the debris, will not be known for probably weeks.

Citizens Dock, which had a lumber barge tied to it, was reported severely damaged, as were fishing boats in the basin. During the surges, the bay seemed to empty like a wash basin, and the harbor entrance appeared as an outgoing river; then the tables would turn, and the basin would fill up and gush over.

Not only water, but fire, started by water causing electrical shorts, took its toll. Leveled were Nichols Pontiac and the Texaco Oil Distributing station and tanks, plus the Union Oil company tanks all south of the city.

The entire downtown section is blocked off, and only those with permits from the Crescent City police department can enter the area. "This," said Police Chief Keyzers, "is limited to people who have business establishments in the area, or other authorized personnel. Even then, they enter at their own risk, he added.

The area is under quarantine, and it is expected to remain so for several days.

Nichols Pontiac, hit by both fire and water, is no longer there.

Lots of debris around the Seaside Hospital but no damage reported.

Local Telephones Silenced, Radio Alerts Are Hampered

By Helen Williams

Radio Station KPLY of Crescent City, 1240 on the area's emergency broadcasting system, retained its power during the hectic hours of last night, but it lost its telephone communication. The series of tidal waves which inundated downtown Crescent City flooded telephone cables causing KPLY's phone to be among many to go dead.

Virginia Deaver, who with her husband, Mason, own and operate the station, had received calls earlier during the night from the city police and the sheriff's office notifying them of the emergency. About 10:00 p.m., people began calling KPLY from places such as Youngstown, Ohio Denver, Colorado; Houston, Texas; Los Angeles; San Francisco and Seattle. These people wanted to know if Crescent City had been affected by the tidal wave. By the time Virginia received the information that the wave had hit and that there were no lives lost or damage done, the phone was dead so she went to a trailer house to place her answering call. Unable to relay her information directly to KGO in San Francisco, she had to go through ABC in Los Angeles.

KPLY received no notice of evacuation for public broadcast and was not aware of the impending disaster until the series of phone calls. If local power had been disrupted, KPLY would have been off the air. Money has already been appropriated to provide the station with emergency power in case of power failure, and the installation has been authorized by the state and federal governments. However, technicalities have delayed the installation. Mason Deaver expressed the opinion that after this current emergency, it won't be long before the station will have its own emergency power equipment.

As the one tidal waved turned out to be a series of surges inflicting havy damage in low-lying areas, KPLY began to receive the first of its hundreds of calls from people requesting assistance in locating missing persons. Reverend John McMath whose home is located across the street from KPLY, 1177 Gelnard Street, volunteered the use of his phone for messages thus terminating the necessity for Virginia to drive to the sheriff's office for news releases. Later, a portable two-way radio system between the McMath's and KPLY aided in speeding the messages over the airwaves.

Throughout the night, the studio was crowded with people waiting for news of missing persons or wishing to assist in some way. "Fortunately," says Virginia, "we were able to aid in locating most of the missing people for whom we had calls. After the second wave, when we got the message to call the national guard into action and to call all doctors and nurses to the hospital, some of these people in our studios assisted in waking up many of the individuals concerned. Most of the called-upon people found it difficult to believe that there was an emergency."

Local ham operators did a good job, according to the Deavers. They got out quite a few reports all over the country, located people and sent messages requested by concerned individuals.

At press time, messages were still pouring into KPLY's studio and were being relayed immediately over the air. The McMath's phone, IN 4-5077, was still being used to receive calls for the station.

Bill Parker, Del Norte County Civilian Defense Director, has been directing most of the activity and gave Virginia most of her bulletins.

BEACH DEVELOPMEN
Join us and Gro

The beachfront development was hard hit.

The Thunderbird Lodge Motel had cars stacked in the drive way at the office entrance.

Crescent City Starts Clean-up Of Tidal Wave's Devastation, Toll In Life, Property Mounts

CRESCENT CITY AMERICAN
VOLUME XXXVIII NUMBER 16 10c PER COPY CRESCENT CITY, CALIFORNIA, TUESDAY, MARCH 31, 1964

PORT FACILITIES WIPED OUT

Tidal Wave Devastates Famed Citizens Dock, Damages Jetty; Sand Accretion "A Problem"

Crescent City harbor, and especially facilities operated directly by the harbor district, or under direct jurisdiction of the harbor district, took a beating by the force of last Saturday morning's tidal wave that left the area in a state of almost total devastation.

Since 1949 when the people of Del Norte County, unaided by any governmental agency, pitched in and built Citizens Dock, more improvement per square foot has occurred in that area than any other part of the county, and the harbor has become known as "The Key to Del Norte's Economy." Modern small boat launching facilities and a new fish wing had recently been added, new buildings have appeared adjacent to the dock, and sand from the district's dredge has been used to build up valuable adjacent lands.

Although the Citizens Dock area is humming with the activity of cleanup operations preparatory to rebuilding in full swing, the wreckage that characterizes the whole area bears mute testimony to the giant blow that, within only a moment, undid the result of years of planning, work and investments.

The lumber wing of Citizens dock is a shambles, and there is only enough piling standing along the main dock approach to the lumber and fish wings to keep the badly sagging floor from falling into the bay. The lumber wing resembles a washboard with planks from the dock floor and piling leaning crazily at all angles. The fish wing, newest portion of the dock, appeared to be in better shape, but to have incurred extensive damage.

The new office building of the Crescent City Harbor Commission had been moved entirely away. The Dock Cafe had washed across the street onto the lumber yards of the Olson shipping company and had come to rest with a sports shop and fish jammed against one side, the Sea Scouts building turned over and on its side against another, and a boat from the bay against still another.

Harbor Commission Chairman Carl Brower said first estimates were that from 22 to 30 commercial fishing boats, including his own were lost. While some of the boats were floated or hurled ashore skindivers were locating others on the bottom of the bay; and some can be restored to valuable use. Lumber stacks from the Olson and Pacific Inland Navigation company yards were scattered over a wide area.

Most of the floor from Sause Brothers Dock, (not currently in use) was uncapped from the piling and deposited on the Crescent City Harbor front. Dutton's Dock appeared to have escaped any major damage.

Considerable damage to the harbor breakwater, full extent of which is not yet determined, has not yet been reported. A federal government contract was recently let for repair of the breakwater, but the amount of the repair under the contract was based on the jetty's condition previous to the tidal wave.

Perhaps symbolical of the damage to the jetty was the fact that after coming into Crescent City, the wave had force enough to move the 25-ton tetrapod at the city's south limits from its foundation. Over 1,900 of the tetrapods were used to strengthen the jetty dog-leg.

Another factor of undetermined possible damage is the amount of sand that may have been deposited in the harbor by the series of surges. A government dredging project of the main harbor and channel has been officially approved, but a large area in the fishboat basin and adjacent to Citizens Dock is the local harbor district's responsibility.

Financing for restoration of Citizens Dock is assured, since it is public property, but until rebuilt, it is totally useless. One fisherman said commercial boats may have to use the port of Eureka until service is restored here.

Special Svc. Set Up For Flood Victims

Carlos Hunsinger, Manager of the social security office in Eureka, and Joe Kycek, field representative of that office, were in Crescent City, Monday, March 30 to check the flood damage here and to see what special services the social security office could offer to help relieve the economic distress of the area.

Mr. Hunsinger stated that his office would give special handling to all social security claims resulting from the flood so as to make payments to the claimants as soon as possible. Persons who may be entitled to receive social security benefits include not only survivors of working people who died in the flood, but also working people over 62 years of age who may now be temporarily unemployed or out of business because of the flood damage.

Persons who believe they may be entitled to benefits should see representatives of the social security office at the office of the California State Employment Service in Crescent City on any Wednesday, their regular visiting day. On Wednesday, April 1, the employees of the social security office will start interviewing claimants at about 10 a.m. in order to try to see everyone who may come in.

Arrangements have been made with Michael Neish, Postmaster in Crescent City, to hold in the Post Office the social security benefit checks of all beneficiaries in the area which cannot be delivered immediately. These next checks covering the month of March, would normally be delivered on about April 3, 1964, and those beneficiaries who have moved as a result of the flood should call for their checks at the Post Office if they do not receive them at that time.

A Terrifying Ride

LaVelle Torgerson was one among many local people subjected to terrifying experiences after the turn of midnight last Saturday morning. Unaware of the approaching halocaust, she rode her trailer house a rugged half mile from its location south of the city into a field, after it was picked up by the tidal wave. She then climbed on top of the trailer and waited until rescued.

CAPTURING the full extent of damage from the tidal wave from the air is impossible, but the above showing an area [illegible] back of Front gives a partial idea. Note buildings in changed positions, some of which are wreckage; cars out of place and other evidences that things are not just right.

Red Cross Moves In, Does Big Job During Wave Emergency

Food, shelter, clothing, are words that are synonymous with the Red Cross. Almost as soon as the last puddle from the catastrophical tidal wave of March 28th was drying up in Crescent City, Calif., the American Red Cross was in action to alleviate the suffering and shock of the disaster's victims.

Headquarters were set up in the Memorial Building at 8th and H Streets and an experienced staff swung into action under the direction of Wally Read, Asst. Director of Disaster Service, Golden Gate Chapter, American Red Cross, San Francisco, Calif. Local volunteers were plentiful and ready and willing to help.

Foremost among its services was the handling of approximately 700 inquiries concerning the welfare of various individuals The inquiries came in lots of 50 to 100, over the telephone and the wireless. Disaster films shown on televisin Saturday night brought a fresh rush of messages of concern. On Sunday, the Red Cross had already answered 300 of these messages.

The fateful wave caused the displacement of a great many elderly people, bachelors in trailers and renters. Stunned families who were wiped out as far as material possessions are concerned, sought assistance at Memorial Hall. Two registered nurses are on duty there to help calm down nervous or emotionally upset victims. On Saturday, food inmthe form of sandwiches, rolls, coffee and milk was fed to the hungry. On Sunday hot meals were available including meat loaf, potatoes, salad, carrot sticks, chili and beans to name a few items.

Some survivors just wanted information or a place to go. Many were transients who had been lodged in motels and being unfamiliar with the town needed directions and aid.

On the stage in the hall are still unwrapped cots, ready to be used when needed. A half dozen cots with blankets sat in front of the stage, some of them having been used already by upset individuals. Actual sleeping accomodations are provided at the county fairgrounds.

Clothing is handled by a group of Seventh Day Adventist women at the church's school on Northcrest Drive. The regular stock of the church's clothing for the needy was soon exhausted and a call was put out by radio KPLY for more donations. Soon, the flood of clothing was so great that there was no place to sort it so the call was retracted for awhile. On Sunday, disaster victims poured into the center for clothing with a large number expected Monday.

The Red Cross, of course, will aid in buying new clothing for the needy. Wally Read says, "We use local merchants as our source of purchasing supplies. We are thus helping the community in two ways. First we provide relief that people need and second, we are helping the local economy." Clothing stores damaged by the wave are expecting to set up temporary quarters so that survivors may purchase new clothing.

Mr. Read says, "We expect that about 200 families will be receiving some kind of assistance. We will help them reestablish their homes by aiding in repairing or rebuilding their homes and by providing furniture. We expect people to do everything they can do themselves and the Red Cross fills in the gap. There is no repayment of our assistance. But, people, in order to receive our assistance, must come to us to apply for it."

Emergency assistance for disaster victims is provided without question upon application. Later when victims wish to reestablish themselves in homes, they work together with the Red Cross in planning how to do it.

Mr. Read, who has been with the Red Cross for 17 years, points out that the Red Cross tried also to provide men on guard duty with nourishment. Members of the National Guard came in shifts to eat at Memorial Hall.

He praised the efforts of a group of teenage boys who employed their Hondas and cars to run messages for the Red Cross. Obtainable were some of the names of the boys and they are Rudy Mercer, Jim Tomlinson, Mike Rhodes, Steve Miller, Jack Morgan, John Ridgeway, Bob Dusenbury, Steve Howard, Steve Justus and Joe Dusenbury. These boys had special armbands downtown. One young man came back from a trip and exclaimed to Mr. Read, "Boy, I almost got shot. The guard didn't know about us boys!"

Wally Read says, "I can't get over how marvelously the community has responded in this disaster. Everyone has been willing to help. And," he says, "As long as there is a victim who needs assistance of any sort, the American Red Cross will not leave Crescent City."

Even as he spoke, a family of three came in, a father, mother and teenage son. Their faces were pale and strained. Immediately upon their entry, they were enfolded into the efficient and friendly arms of the organization known as the American Red Cross.

Clausen Asks Silver Dollar Continuation

Washington, D. C. ——Congressman Don H. Clausen today defended the silver dollar as a tradition of the West and accused the U.S. Treasury of causing a "run on the Treasury" to deplete the silver dollar supply.

Clausen joined other Western Congressmen in attempting to preserve the silver dollar from extinction by attempting to have a supply minted.

The House of Representatives refused to allocate funds to mint new silver dollars, none of which have been made since 1935.

Clausen charged that the Treasury Department caused a depletion of the silver dollar supply by:

—"proposing that the minting of silver dollars be dropped," creating a demand for them by cin collectors and speculators.

—"offering old silver dollars for 'sale', "increasing the demand.

—and "by selling them openly to all comers....not just to those seeking to redeem silver certificates."

Silver certificates are the type of one dollar bills printed by the government until November of last year. Each of these bears the legend: "This certifies that there is on deposit in the Treasury of the United States of America one dollar in silver payable to the bearer on demand."

Clausen Asks Federal Disaster Area Designation, Death Toll At 10, Rebuilding Is Planned

At a special board of supervisors meeting in the courthouse yesterday afternoon Congressman Don Clausen told representatives of various local governmental agencies that he has telegraphed President Johnson asking that he recognize Crescent City and vicinity as an emergency federal disaster area.

Clausen said his inspection of the area reveals that conditions here are "horrible."

Among federal representatives attending the meeting were General Frye and Col. Robert Allen of the army Engineers, and Ralph Burns, Director of Federal Emergency Planning.

In rapid fire order, Burns said as soon as President Johnson declares the area, he would authorize the army engineers to proceed with local aids. He added however, he would need requests from the board of supervisors and city council for available aids.

The board then adopted a resolution requesting the aids, and city councilmen attending held an immediate emergency session and presented the same request. Burns, in turn, authorized the army engineers to move in immediately upon being advised of the President's declaration.

The aids would include cleanup, or reimbursements for cleanups where necessary for health and safety reasons, and repair or replacement of public facilities. These include repair of the ocean outfall of the sewer system, replacement of a portion of the seawall which was washed from the city's harbor frontage, and repair or replacement of the devastated harbor facilities.

Both Burns and Gen. Frye were highly complementary of the manner in which local people have pitched in to make great strides already evident in the cleanup job. "And," said Burns, "the conservative manner in which requests are made here is amazing."

From a local source, Crescent City Realtor Bill Mason, who played a major role in the original building of Citizens Dock (by the people without help from any source), came the following comment:

"I see here the same spirit that built the dock in 1949; the same unselfishness on the part of so many willing to help. And, I am amazed by the number of business men and women, some of whom have lost all of their savings to date, who are not discouraged, and who say they will rebuild."

Holding out a hope to business men is the fact that officials of the Federal Small Business Administration will hold an all-day session in the old High School building beginning at 9 o'clock this morning. Purpose is to confer with local business men needing emergency loans.

Also, late yesterday the Bank of America headquarters in San Francisco wired the Crescent City American is working closely with the SBA looking toward disaster loans.

Meanwhile, the death toll from drownings in the Crescent City area climbed to 10, and 14 people are still listed as missing, according to Civilian Defense Director William Parker. This does not include Oran Magruder, widely known founder of Magruders Redwood Manufacturing and Gift Shop, who died of a heart attack during the disaster.

Neither do the missing include Sgt. Donald McClure, 36, of Requa Airforce Base, who was washed out to sea from the mouth of the Klamath River.

The dead were identified, as follows:

Mr. and Mrs. Earl Edwards and Mr. and Mrs. William Clawson, all in their 50's and all of Crescent City; Joan Fields, 25, Crescent City; Adolph Arrigoni, 70, Crescent City; James Parks, 60, Crescent City; LaVelle Hillsbery, 34, and two children 10-months old William Eugene and 3-year old Bonita, son and daughter of Mr. and Mrs. William Wright of Crescent City.

Meanwhile, rough estimates of the monetary damage ran a wide range from $20 million to $50 million, with a certainty outstanding that the full extent of the damage will not be known for weeks.

Percentage wise, the disaster from a tidal wave in Crescent City that was triggered by an earthquake in Anchorage, Alaska, was far greater than the earthquake itself.

LOCAL FIRES FOLLOW TIDAL WAVE

Escaped gasoline, sparked by tidal wave of early Saturday morning, caused electrical shorts were the main factor that caused destruction of the Shell Oil company bulk plant and tanks, and Nichols Pontiac just south of Oil plant and tanks.

Fire Chief Lyle Griffin said men and equipment of the Crescent Fire Protection District answered the alarm at 2:05 a.m., but were blocked with several feet of water between that had rolled in on U.S. Highway 101. "Until we encountered the water," he said, "we did not know about the wave."

When the department finally did reach the scene, they were trapped for a time with gasoline that had ignited from a short then, they were ordered away because of a new tidal wave alert.

Also at 2 o'clock Sunday morning, and perhaps because of wave shattered telephone service, the home of Haskel Smith at 2465 Hodge Avenue in the Bertsch Tract was a total fire loss.

"Smith got his wife and six children from the house," Griffin said, "but the alarm was delayed until a neighbor had taken his car and contacted a California Highway Patrolman directing traffic around the Crescent City disaster area."

The patrolman radioed in the alarm, Griffin added, but by the time 17 firemen who answered the call arrived, the house was too far gone to save. Cause of the fire is unknown. Both the house and furnishings were covered by insurance, he said.

Explains Reason For Quarantine

County Sanitarian Joe Creisler said yesterday that the quarantine against people entering the downtown area has been the occasion from a great many inquiries from people who erroneously think the water is contaminated.

"There is nothing wrong with the water," Creisler explained. "There would be a danger, if anyone ate contaminated food found in the area, but one of the main reasons is safety; that is, the condition of the buildings, some of which are weakened and may collapse, thus posing an accident hazard.

FULL COVERAGE "TIDAL WAVE" IN THIS ISSUE

Because over 2,500 copies of the special 4-page tidal wave edition of the Crescent City American were sold out in rapid order, and there are requests for hundreds more, we have republished the edition and are carrying it as an added section in this issue.

Since the wave left the greatest disaster in Del Norte county's history in its wake, we are not publishing some of our special features this week in order to leave room for additional articles and photographs depicting the great tragedy.

Power Co. Opens At 1054 Northcrest

Pacific Power and Light company, flooded from its office at 270 "I" Street, has opened an emergency office at 1054 Northcrest Drive, Phones IN 4-2115 and IN 4-4129. Local Manager Carl Pyles said crews have caught up on emergency repairs and they are ready to reconnect damaged houses as soon as they have been cleared by inspectors.

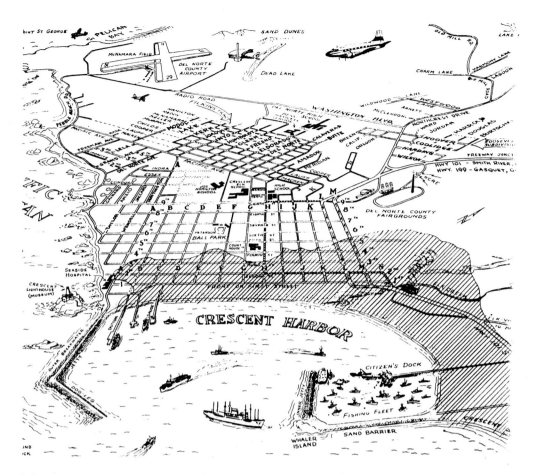

Map of Crescent City showing the extent of the waves on the downtown and outlying areas (hatched lines). CRESCENT CITY PRINTING CO. VIA WALLACE H. GRIFFIN

Citizen's Dock in Crescent Harbor was a shambles. There was only enough pilings standing along the main dock approach to the lumber and fish wings to keep the badly sagging floor from falling into the bay. DNHS WALT HARRIS COLLECTION

Looking North.

During the downtown reconstruction, 2nd Street was abandoned and a plaza and memorial fountain was built. The county library building is right behind the memorial fountain. The sign on the post below *Tsunami Landing* denotes the high water mark of the tsunami. DNHS

Looking South.

Monument to those who died on March 28, 1964.
CRESCENT CITY—DEL NORTE COUNTY
CHAMBER OF COMMERCE

Washington

Two people were injured and two more suffered heart attacks. Bridge and road damages were at least $80,000. One fishing boat was wrecked. Several skiffs and fishing nets were lost ($4,000). At least 16 homes were damaged, including three destroyed. Nine trailers were damaged and three cars were lost. One mile of sea bulkhead was lost.

A grandmother in Seattle heard of the possible tsunami and called her daughter who was vacationing with her daughter, Patty (age 11), at Kalaloch Beach, Jefferson County. The daughter and an 11-year-old boy were camping on the beach. The mother reached them five to 10 minutes before the wave. The boy went immediately to higher ground but the girl wanted to get her sleeping bag and pup tent. The mother grabbed the girl and headed for higher ground when she heard the water and logs coming. They reached a tree at the base of the 40-foot scrub covered embankment when the wave struck. The water reached their knees. After the wave receded, they attempted to climb higher. The second wave still reached their ankles although they were five feet higher. All escaped without injury (*Seattle Daily Times*, March 30, 1964).

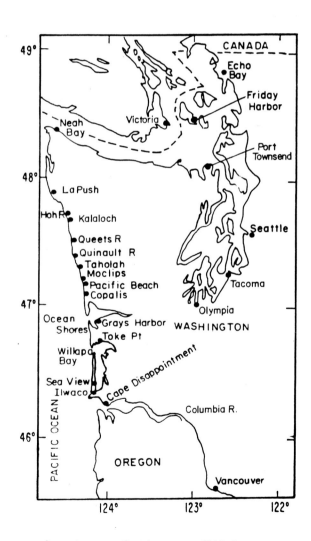

Location map for the state of Washington.

Oregon

Four children drowned and one woman suffered a fatal heart attack. Bridges, houses, trailers, cars, motel units and seas walls were destroyed along the coast. Damage estimates are uncertain but appear to be between $750,000 and $1 million. Most of the communities did not receive any warning.

California

There were 12 fatalities, excluding the death of a Wilmington longshoreman killed when a cable on a crane broke and dropped a loaded pallet on him. Twelve were injured in Crescent City during the early part of the disaster. Damage in California probably exceeded $17 million. Crescent City was the worst affected with about $15 million worth of damage. About $1 million in damages occurred inside San Francisco bay due to currents—a major source of damage on the southern California Coast. Late arriving surges also caused one death and considerable damage. Because of its proximity and source region orientation, this event is perhaps the most damaging tsunami to be expected for northern California and can serve as a design tsunami.

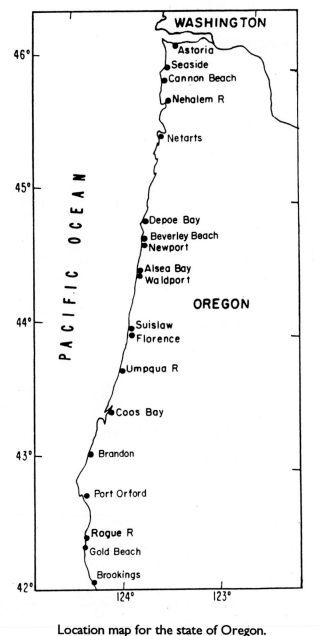

Location map for the state of Oregon.

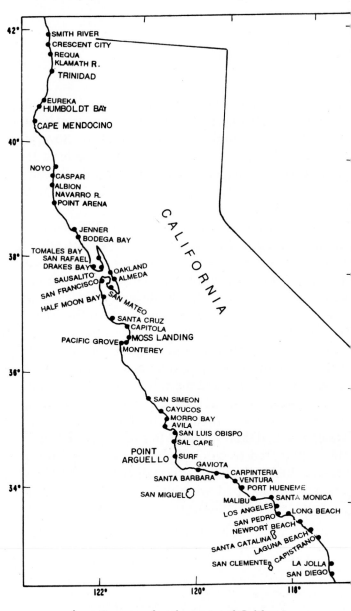

Location map for the state of California.

Damage along the West Coast of the United States as a result of the tsunami on March 28, 1964, caused by the Alaska earthquake of March 27, 1964.*

Aberdeen, WA—three log rafts broke loose, trailers flooded.

Avila, CA—boats broke mooring, $2,000 damage.

Belfair, WA—water flooded highway.

Bodega Bay, CA—one drowned.

Boone Creek, WA—bridge damaged, $500 damage at Iron Springs Resort.

Brandon, OR—log boom and boats broke free.

Brookings, OR—Coast Guard boat damaged.

Cannon Beach, OR—bridge and motel unit moved .3 km inland, $230,000 damage

Caspar, CA—highway flooded.

Cayucos, CA—parking lot flooded.

Charleston, OR—chartered boat and fishing boat sunk.

Coos Bay, OR—$20,000 in damage.

Copalis, WA—small bridge destroyed and $5,000 damage in town. Four mobile campers overturned.

Depoe Bay, OR—$5,000 in damage, four children killed while camping at Beverly Beach.

Florence, OR—$50,000 in damage.

Grays Harbor, WA—eight autos lost, nine trailers damaged, five houses damaged or destroyed.

Gearhart, OR—home flooded, cabin left in road.

Half Moon Bay, CA—boat sunk, cabin left in road.

Humboldt Bay, CA—street flooded.

Ilwaco, WA—minor damage.

Joe Creek, WA—bridge damaged.

Kalaloch Beach, WA—two children rescued.

Klamath River, CA—one killed, $4,000 damage to boat dock and boats at Requa.

La Push, WA—boat wrecked.

Long Beach Harbor, CA—eight docks destroyed, $100,000 value.

Los Angeles County Harbor, CA—$75,000 damage to harbor sides.

Los Angeles, CA—$200,000 damage to six boat slips, fuel dock damaged, one fatality.

Marin County, CA—$1 million damage.

Moclips, WA—bulkhead washed out, $6,000 damage to eight houses, road damaged.

Monterey, CA—small boats broke loose, $1,000 damage.

Morro Bay, CA—fuel dock lost, $10,000 damage.

Newport, OR—1.9m of retaining wall destroyed.

Noyo, CA—100 fishing boats damaged, 10 sunk, $250,000 to $1 million damage.

Pacific Beach, WA—$12,000 damage to houses, one injured.

Rogue River, OR—$30,000 damage.

San Rafael, CA—$77,500 damage to boats and berthing facilities.

Santa Monica, CA—boat sunk.

Sausalito, CA—$100,000 damage to floating structures and boats at Clipper Yacht Harbor.

Seaside, OR—one died of heart attack, $41,000 in damage to city, $250,000 in private property, four trailers, 10-12 houses, two bridges damaged.

Smith River, CA—$6,000 damage to floating structures.

Taholah, WA—$1,000 damage, skiffs destroyed, fish nets lost.

Tomales Bay, CA—$6,000 damage to pier.

Umpaqua River, OR—$5,000 damage.

Waldport-Alsea, OR—$20,000 damage done to rafts and docks.

Westport, WA—bridge damaged.

Wilapa Bay, WA—three homes flooded, $2,000 damaged.

Wreck Creek, WA—$5,000 damage.

Yaquina Bay, OR—$5,000 damage.

*From a table in the NOAA report, Documentation No. 29 (see bibliography).

AFTERSHOCKS

The Alaska earthquake not only affected Alaska and the west coast of North America, but many other areas of the world. Over 700 ground-water wells in practically every state in the Union recorded some fluctuations in their water level some time after the March 27 quake. Water-level fluctuations were also recorded in streams, reservoirs, ponds and lakes throughout the world.

The largest fluctuation in a well was 28 feet registered near Belle Fourche, South Dakota. Wells in Alabama, Florida, Georgia, Illinois, Missouri and Pennsylvania registered fluctuations of more than 10 feet. As far away as Puerto Rico, a well recorded a 3.4 foot fluctuation.

Well fluctuations were also recorded as far away as Libya, South Africa, The Philippines, Australia, Belgium, Britain and throughout Canada.

Seismic activity along the Gulf of Mexico and in the bayous of Louisiana, after the Alaska quake, were large enough to cause some destruction in a local lake.

A few of the major aftershocks produced some water well fluctuations throughout the continent between March 27 and April 4, but to a much smaller degree. The aftershocks continued from March 30 to April 7. One seismic station in Anchorage counted 560 local shocks between these dates.

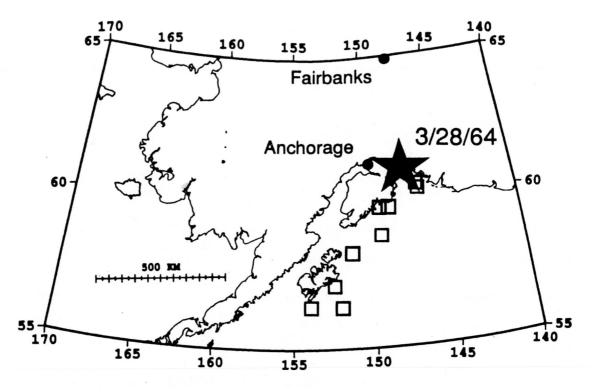

Main shock and largest aftershocks of the 1964 Alaska earthquake. The main shock, represented by the large star, had a moment magnitude (Mw) of 9.2. Aftershocks of magnitude 6.0 and larger are shown by boxes. The aftershock region defines the rupture zone, which was more than 700 kilometers long.

EARTHQUAKE ALASKA- ARE WE PREPARED?, U.S. GEOLOGICAL SURVEY, OPEN-FILE REPORT 94-218, 1994

Destruction was great in the downtown area of Kodiak and the small-boat harbor. Many fishing boats were tossed hundreds of feet on shore by the seismic wave. KHS

Wreckage of the Portage Creek bridge #3 on the Seward-Anchorage Highway and the Alaska Railroad bridge. COE

Destruction at Whittier. COE

The boardwalk at Seldovia was inundated by tides due to a 3.5 tectonic subsidence. COE

Cordova was left high and dry due to the tectonic uplift. COE

Union Oil Company tanks burning at Valdez. COE

The new townsite of Valdez was located at Mineral Point, about four miles by road west of the devastated community. It is located on bedrock that is not susceptible to underwater slides. COE

What's left of a hotel in Valdez. COE

Remains of a homestead on Turnagain Arm. COE

Montague Island is in Prince William Sound. It suffered extensive subsidence and uplift relative to sea level. This view shows a sunken forest in June 1964. COE

Remains of cabins at Chenega. COE

The railroad facilities at Seward were totally destroyed. COE

Some of the destruction at Seward had been cleared up by May 1964 when this photo was taken, but alot was left to do. COE

Fourth Avenue in Anchorage. STEWART'S PHOTO SHOP, ANCHORAGE

After the earthquake Turnagain Heights resembled the badlands of South Dakota. The Bootlegger Cove Clay that underlaid the Heights was greatly distorted. COE

Bibliography

Brochures, pamphlets

1. *The Severity of an Earthquake*, U.S. Geological Survey, Denver, Colo., 1991.
2. *Earthquakes*, U.S. Geological Survey, Denver, Colo., 1991.
3. *The Next Big Earthquake in Southern Alaska May Come Sooner Than You Think*, U.S. Geological Survey, Anchorage, Alaska.
4. *Operation Helping Hand The Armed Forces React to Earthquake Disaster*, Alaskan Command.
5. Various issues of the *Anchorage Times* and *Anchorage Daily News*.

Books

1. Engle, Eloise, *Earthquake The Story of Alaska's Good Friday Disaster*, The John Day Company, New York, 1966.
2. Griffin, Wallace, *Crescent City's Dark Disaster*, Crescent City Printing Co., Inc., Crescent City, Calif., 1984.
3. Lander, James. F., Patricia A. Lockridge, Michael J. Kozuch, *Tsunamis Affecting the West Coast of the United States*, 1806-1992, U.S. Dept. of Commerce, NOAA, 1993.

DEATH TOLL

Crescent City, Calif.	*11*
Newport, Oregon	*4*
Valdez	*30*
Chenega	*25*
Kodiak	*19*
Whittier	*11*
Seward	*13*
Anchorage	*9*
Total	*114*

ANCHORAGE DEAD

Turnagain
Perry Mead III – 12 years old
Merrell Mead – 2 years old
Mrs. Virginia Knight

Falling Wreckage
Clayton Baker
Gary Lynn Kleparek
J.J. Martines
Marie Rustigan
Lee Styer

Airport
William Taylor

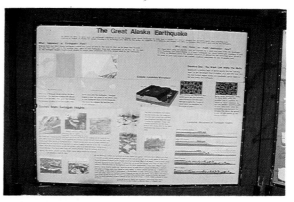

Display at Earthquake Park on West Northern Lights Boulevard above Turnagain.

The Destructive Power of Mother Nature

The Turnagain Heights
slide. COE & ASL, U.S. ARMY COE,
PCA 100-168

Army National Guard in Anchorage. BOB REEVE COLLECTION

About the Author

Stan Cohen is a native of West Virginia and a graduate geologist from West Virginia University. He spent several summers working in Alaska before the 1964 earthquake and many years as a consulting geologist in Montana. Since 1976, he has owned Pictorial Histories Publishing Company and has authored or co-authored 78 books and published over 300. His Alaska titles include the following: *The Great Alaska Pipeline, The Trail of '42, Alcan and Canol, Gold Rush Gateway, The Streets Were Paved With Gold, Highway on the Sea, Yukon River Steamboats, The Forgotten War* (four volumes), *Rails Across the Tundra* and *White Pass and Yukon Route.* He lives in Missoula, Montana, with his wife, Anne.

Why Earthquakes are Inevitable in Alaska

Geologists know that the surface of the Earth is made up of a dozen or so large fragments called "plates." Most of these plates are more than 1,000 miles across and are more than 40 miles thick. The Earth has had moving plates for at least several billion years, and these will continue to shift in the future. The plates move steadily, but slowly, past each other at rates currently up to four inches per year. Most earthquakes occur at the boundaries where plates are sliding past each other, but some are internal to plates. If it were possible to stop the movement of the plates, there would be no earthquakes, but because the plates will continue moving as they have for billions of years, there undoubtedly will be future earthquakes. Southern and southeastern Alaska lie at the boundary between two plates, the North American plate on the north and east and the Pacific plate on the south and west.

There are three ways that plates can move relative to each other:

1) **The plates move toward each other.** This is the situation in southern Alaska and along the Aleutian Islands where the Pacific plate dives beneath the North American plate. The Earth's largest earthquakes, such as the 1964 Alaskan one, generally occur where plates are moving toward each other. Another result of the convergence of plates are volcanoes, such as we have on the Alaska Peninsula and on the Aleutian Islands.

2) **The plates slide by each other.** This is the geologic setting offshore of southeastern Alaska, where the North American plate and the Pacific plate slide past each other on the Fairweather–Queen Charlotte fault. The same type of movement on the San Andreas fault in California is what causes many damaging earthquakes there.

3) **The plates move away from each other.** This situation occurs mostly in the deep ocean, and does not typically generate large earthquakes.